⬛ The American Film Institute

Writing Great

Screenplays

For Film and TV

Dona Cooper

MACMILLAN • USA

First Edition

Macmillan General Reference
A Simon & Schuster Macmillan Company
1633 Broadway
New York, NY 10019-6785

An Arco Book

MACMILLAN is a registered trademark of Macmillan, Inc.
ARCO is a registered trademark of Prentice-Hall, Inc.

Library of Congress Cataloging-in-Publication Data

Cooper, Dona.
    Writing great screenplays for film and TV / Dona Cooper.
      p. cm.
    At head of title: The American Film Institute.
    "An Arco book."
    ISBN 0-671-84783-X
    1. Motion picture authorship. 2. Television authorship.
3. Motion picture plays--Technique. 4. Television plays--Technique.
I. American Film Institute. II. Title.
PN1996.C813   1994
808.2'3--dc20   93-44339
                                                       CIP

Manufactured in the United States of America

10   9   8   7   6   5

Dedication

To Oliver Hailey, who helped me appreciate both the art and craft of writing.

Acknowledgments

I would like to express deep thanks to:

Jan Wildman, for her creative insights, clear thinking, and dedication to the cause

Linda Cappel, for the book's illustrations, as well as the many "invisible" solutions she invented

Barbara Gilson, for her patience and wisdom

Candace Kopel, for her insight and support

Sarah Ban Breathnach and Marcia Bartusiak, for sharing their war stories

Colette Wilson and Jan Cerveny, for their help and humor

Jean Firstenberg, Ron Silverman, Beth Taylor, and Chris Craig, for the opportunity and encouragement

And always, my husband, Arthur Popov, and my sister Connie Cooper, for their constant love and support

CONTENTS

Contents

THE AMERICAN FILM INSTITUTE

*T*he American Film Institute was created in 1967 as an independent, national, nonprofit organization by the National Endowment for the Arts to "preserve the heritage and advance the art of film and television in the United States." Through a series of interrelated programs emanating from its offices in Washington, D.C., New York City, and Los Angeles, the institute conducts activities around the country that work toward the achievement of its primary goals:

- to increase recognition and understanding of the moving image as an art form
- to assure preservation of the art form
- to identify, develop, and encourage new talent

The American Film Institute

Jean Picker Firstenberg
Director

James Hindman
Deputy Director

Bruce Neiner
Associate Director
Finance and Administration

Susan Dutton
Director
Development and Public Affairs

Ken Wlaschin
Director
Creative Affairs

Tess Martin
Director
Production Training Programs

Greg Lukow
Director, Administration
Center for Film
and Video Preservation

Nick DeMartino
Director
Advanced Technology
Programs

Rod Merl
Director, Administration
Center for Advanced Film
and Television Studies

Ron Silverman
Dean of Studies
Center for Advanced
Film and Television Studies

Dezso Magyar
Director
Center for Advanced
Film and Television Studies

History of The American Film Institute

"We will create an American Film Institute, bringing together leading artists of the film industry, outstanding educators, and young men and women who wish to pursue this 20th century art form as their life's work."

With these words, President Lyndon Johnson signed the National Arts and Humanities Act of 1965. The legislation created the National Endowment for the Arts (NEA) and, in turn, the American Film Institute was established as an independent, nonprofit organization dedicated to promoting the art of the moving image: to preserve the film classics of the past, advocate an appreciation of film and television in the present, and help to train the filmmaker of the future.

The institute's first chairman was Gregory Peck, and George Stevens, Jr., was named the founding director. Initial funding came from three sources (each at the $1.3 million level): the National Endowment for the Arts; the Ford Foundation; and the member companies of the Motion Picture Association of the Board of Trustees from private, foundation, and corporate sources.

Setting an immediate pattern for the AFI's activities, one of the first projects undertaken by the AFI was a "rescue" operation to locate and preserve 250 rare and historically valuable firms. Since then the AFI film collection at the Library of Congress has totaled close to 25,000 motion pictures, spanning the spectrum from Laurel & Hardy films to *Lost Horizon*.

In 1969 the AFI established its conservatory, the Center for Advanced Film Studies, at Greystone, the Doheny mansion in Beverly Hills. Among the crop of young filmmakers who studied at the Conservatory during its first year were Jeremy Paul Kagan (*The Chosen, The Adventures of Natty Gann*); Caleb Deschanel (*The Black Stallion, The Right Stuff, The Natural*); Matthew Robbins (*The Sugarland Express, Batteries Not Included*); and Paul Schrader (*Taxi Driver, Mishima*).

History of The American Film Institute

In Washington the AFI opened its exhibition program at the National Gallery in 1970, moving in 1973 to its own theater at the John F. Kennedy Center for the Performing Arts. By 1970 the AFI's publications program was underway with the *AFI Guide to College Courses in Film and Television*, the *AFI Catalog Project*, and a series of oral histories of filmmaking: *American Film*, debuted in October, 1975. The AFI's first feature-length Film-on-Film was *Directed by John Ford*, made in 1968 by Peter Bogdanovich, three years before he became internationally known for *The Last Picture Show*.

John Cassavetes became the first Filmmaker-in-Residence at the Center in 1972; in 1973, the AFI began what has become perhaps its best-known activity with the presentation of the first Life Achievement Award to John Ford. The Life Achievement Award has become the highest honor a filmmaker or actor can receive, and the annual ceremony is telecast worldwide. Subsequent recipients have included Fred Astaire, James Cagney, Frank Capra, Bette Davis, Henry Fonda, Lillian Gish, Alfred Hitchcock, John Huston, Gene Kelly, Jack Lemmon, Gregory Peck, Barbara Stanwyck, James Stewart, Orson Welles, Billy Wilder, William Wyler, Sir David Lean, Kirk Douglas, Sidney Poitier, and, in 1993, Elizabeth Taylor.

One of the most notable programs run under the AFI auspices is the Directing Workshop for Women, which, beginning in 1974, has given dozens of professional women the chance to direct motion pictures. Lee Grant, Randa Haines, Nancy Malone, Neema Barnett, and Jan Eliasberg are just a few of those who have honed their directorial abilities under this program.

George Stevens, Jr., resigned as director of the AFI in 1979. His successor was Jean Picker Firstenberg, who has served for the past thirteen years, overseeing the AFI's continued expansion, which has included a major improvement of facilities. In 1981 the AFI acquired the former campus of Immaculate Heart College on Western Avenue in Los Angeles. Occupying four buildings spread over eight acres, the campus provides a spacious home for the institute. More than 1,500 men and women have received training at the conservatory, now called The Center for Advanced Film and Television Studies, including Bob Mandell, Michael Dinner, David Lynch, John McTiernan, Jon Avnet, Marshall Herskovitz, Ed Zwick, and Amy Heckerling. In 1985, the Center became the first film school to be accredited by the National Association of Schools of Art and Design. That same year the AFI became the first art institute to be included in the California Education Facilities Authority Pooled Bond Program, which infused the institute with $6.7 million from the tax-free bond issue to refinance the acquisition and renovation of the campus.

The AFI has continued to encourage new filmmakers with grants and programs that have steadily extended into new areas, and television is now firmly within the AFI's purview. Since 1981 the institute has sponsored the National Video Festival and its touring program of new and innovative works, and operates a Television Writers' Workshop and the state-of-the-art Sony Video Center on the Los Angeles campus. AFI graduates have produced numerous telefeatures, including *LBJ: The Early Years*, by Peter Werner; *The Burning Bed*, by Jon Avnet; and *Special Bulletin*, by Marshall Herskovitz and Ed Zwick, all of which have won numerous awards.

The AFI continually strives to showcase new works by emerging filmmakers, most visibly through the annual AFI/Los Angeles International Film Festival, which is rapidly becoming one of America's most respected film festivals. The AFI Independent Award—the Maya Deren—was created in 1986 to recognize the contributions of independent film and video artists and to raise public awareness of their work.

In September 1989 the institute celebrated the approaching twenty-fifth anniversary of the establishment of the NEA with a "Back to the Rose Garden" event in Washington, D.C., at which President George Bush said: "For almost a quarter of a century, the American Film Institute has nurtured and celebrated the art of the moving image. In doing so, it has had an immense impact on the mind and soul of America."

Preserving, training, and celebrating; for more than twenty years the American Film Institute has sought to fulfill its mandate to support this greatest of American art forms, the art of the moving image.

INTRODUCTION

I used to work in live theater, where performers often regale each other with variations of the classic "Actor's Nightmare." They dramatically describe the horrifying sensation of finding themselves on stage, midperformance, and suddenly having no idea what play they're supposed to perform! They all react differently in their panic; some ramble, some freeze, and some simply run screaming from the stage. Then—thank heavens!—they wake up and realize the agony is only imaginary; the nightmare is only a dream.

Now I work in Hollywood, where I discovered that there's also a "Screenwriter's Nightmare." It usually goes something like this:

You get a great idea for a script. You're eager, excited, and convinced that it will make a great movie. You jot down ideas that come easily at first, but eventually you begin to slow down. Something's wrong. What should you do? Ignore the sensation? Start over again?

Often what happens is that you turn to the plethora of books or seminars available, where you're quickly assured that there are specific formulas that work for any script. Just put "these" events into "that" order and, voilà, you've got yourself a hit screenplay! So you sit yourself back at the keyboard, happily convinced that the worst is behind you.

Usually it's not. Somehow the one-size-fits-all formulas don't fit your ideas, and the foolproof systems manage to fail. Panic, frustration, even paralysis set in. Now what do you do? Toss out your idea or abandon the formula? Give up on your script or trudge wearily to the end? Either way, you're unhappy with the outcome and never really sure whether the problem is your idea, your technique, your discipline, or simply a complete and utter lack of talent.

Wouldn't it be great if you woke up and found out it was all a bad dream? However, chances are that you won't, because, unlike the Actor's Nightmare, this one happens all the time.

I should know. I've been teaching screenwriting for several years now, and everywhere I go I meet talented but discouraged writers who are confused, frustrated, and even angry. They're tired of being taught rules that sound good but prove to be of little practical use. They're fed up with conventional wisdom that makes even the process of writing unsatisfying, while still not resulting in the professional success they crave.

Introduction

Meanwhile, I've worked with hundreds of executives, producers, and directors who grow more and more alarmed at the difficulty of finding exciting, compelling screenplays. Each weekend they drag home piles of scripts searching for the next great hit, only to read material that seems so predictable it feels almost as if it's been cloned.

The problem is not just that formulaic writing makes for boring reading, but for boring films and television as well. "Hollywood is starving for good material!" screams one trade paper article after another, while box office slumps and TV ratings declines suggest that audiences agree. Yet scripts that follow such formulas continue to cross my desk by the hundreds each year. If the rules and conventions are so effective, why are so many scripts disappointing? Why do most screenplays fail?

Because the formulaic approach doesn't work. After reading more than 10,000 scripts over the course of my career, I can tell you categorically that there are no specifics that work for every screenplay. What is true, however, is that there are fundamental emotional and logical processes that audiences employ to make sense of any story; there is also a crucial relationship between those audience dynamics and the components of a screenplay. Once you understand both those dynamics and their relation to screenwriting, you can begin to use craft imaginatively to express your unique vision rather than as a mold into which you must force your ideas.

That's why I decided to write this book. It's based on the course I teach at the American Film Institute's Center for Advanced Film and Television Studies, and it is the result of my experience during more than twenty years in film, television, and theater. In this book we're going to take a different approach to screenwriting, one that is not only more exciting, satisfying, and productive but more commercially viable as well.

Rather than assuming that successful screenplays contain specific elements whose placement and contents never vary, we'll approach them as we would baking a cake. Virtually every cake uses the same ingredients—butter, sugar, flour, and eggs. What you need to be a good baker is not to know how to use one magic recipe that never changes, but to have a deep, visceral understanding of how each ingredient performs its function and how to change proportions to achieve the results you want.

In this book, we're going to focus on the ingredients of a script. What are the fundamental components of a screenplay? How do they interact? Which cinematic conventions are optional, and which are essential to making successful emotional contact with the viewer?

Introduction

The dynamics we're going to explore are true for any form of cinematic storytelling, whether you want to write for features, network TV, or cable. We'll go back to the very essence of the storytelling process and figure out for ourselves what sensations make a story experience satisfying for the audience, and how those dynamics are addressed by craft. The material is structured to begin with an in-depth presentation of "whys" before exploring the "hows," bringing both the internal and external challenges of screenwriting to your conscious awareness. The goal is to help you develop an "educated gut," which means having clear access to your creative instincts as well as having enough command of craft to express those impulses in a way your audience understands.

So if you've been suffering through the dreaded Screenwriter's Nightmare, take heart. Whether you want to write the zaniest comic escapade or the most poignant drama, this book can help give you back the clarity, confidence, and excitement needed to bring your cinematic vision to life.

ONE

Films as Roller Coasters

You sit down. The room goes dark. The film begins. The level of your involvement may start at "ground zero," but if something catches your interest, you become curious. If something about the story touches you emotionally, soon you're hooked. If the story continues to work its magic, the overall pattern of your emotional reactions becomes more and more intense. Your heart may pound as the climax approaches, soaring with hope or plummeting with despair. But however the story resolves itself, your tension subsides, and the cumulative experience leaves you spent, but satisfied, in a pleasurable and almost physical way.

Isn't that what it feels like to watch a great movie? Wouldn't you love to write screenplays that provoke such compelling sensations in your audience?

Trying to create that kind of emotional reaction is the great challenge of screenwriting. However, most screenwriting approaches handicap you by focusing your attention on the rational sequence of events rather than the emotional build. Such methods are often represented by linear diagrams, some even indicating what sequence, or by which page number, key events should occur.

Films as Roller Coasters

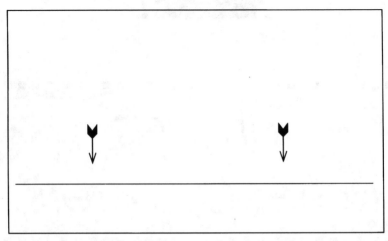

Linear Structure with Key Moments

Not only do I believe such linear prototypes are an inaccurate depiction of the ideal story experience, I think such images actually work against your chance of creating a compelling screenplay. The reason is that while designing a logically cohesive plotline is certainly part of writing a great screenplay, focusing exclusively on the rational progression of events is too one-dimensional to create the results you want. Logic and emotions are different things; a well-constructed legal argument can be dry as dust, while a rambling and almost incoherent mother can break your heart as she tries to explain the accident that killed her child.

So what you must focus on is creating a compelling emotional build of tension and release, because it is that overall experience for which audiences hunger, and it is what ultimately determines whether viewers will find your story emotionally satisfying or not.

As a result, rather than thinking of your cinematic story as a linear construction, I suggest that you begin thinking of it as a two-dimensional roller coaster.

In terms of the cinematic experience, what is going on here? What exactly do these two lines represent?

The bottom line reflects the rational, logical progression of information that the plot conveys to the audience, while the upper line suggests the resulting emotional reaction you want viewers to have. For example, when the story begins, viewers start at a neutral emotional level because they have no information about the plot. Their interest will remain flat until at least one aspect of the story provokes some curiosity; then, if the story begins to

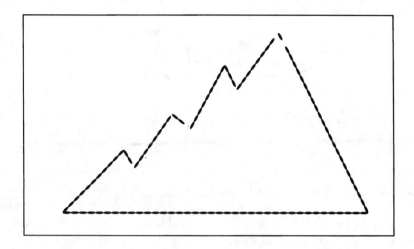

intrigue them, the intensity of their emotional reaction begins to build. The more their emotions are aroused, the more eager they are to know what's going to happen. Maybe a surprise suddenly spurs their interest, or a slow, gentle scene allows them to feel a momentary sense of calm, but the overall pattern of their emotional reaction continues to rise higher and higher. Finally it climaxes; then internal tension begins to subside.

There are several reasons I like the roller-coaster analogy. One is that it captures the sense of thrust, power, build, and intensity that a good story experience must have. It also gives you a tangible, visual image to help focus your creative energies; by envisioning the height of that segment of the roller coaster you want to create, you have a tangible, two-dimensional gauge to aim for, which keeps the desired emotional impact in clear focus. Suddenly it's not enough to decide what will be the next major event in your story; you also need to ask yourself, How do I make this scene intense enough to rise high enough for this part of my story?

Most important, the roller-coaster image graphically conveys the first big secret of successful screenwriting: The cinematic story experience is not just composed of the words you put on the paper (or the resulting sights and sounds that may end up on the screen one day), but also the audience's emotional reaction to that information. Your goal is to write screenplays that provide such a compelling pattern of emotional highs and lows that anyone reading your script can easily imagine an audience also enjoying the ride.

Cinematic roller coasters are composed of five major elements—structure, plot, characters, momentum, and style. Each of these will be examined in more detail in later chapters, but here is a quick overview to give you a sense of these five core components, how they function, and how they interact.

 *I. Structure*

The first and most prominent component of a screenplay is *structure*, the overall design or track of the roller coaster. The function of structure is to provide the comprehensive, "big picture" ride that determines whether your audience will experience a satisfying build to climax and release.

The easiest way to understand structure is to imagine it as the pattern or design of emotional ups and downs that the audience experiences while watching your story. It's almost as if you could hook up EKGs to the bodies of your viewers; when they feel an intense emotion the needle will leap up and when they become bored the needle will descend. By the end of the story, the graph will reflect the exact shape of their emotional reaction. That resulting pattern is what's represented by the roller coaster's design, which is the structure of your story.

The generic version of the cinematic roller coaster can be represented by a simple triangle that is the essential shape of any story:

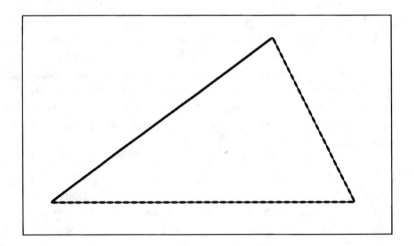

Films as Roller Coasters

However, not all roller coasters are constructed in a linearly diagonal way. For example, here is a kind of "meandering grapevine" roller coaster from a character piece like *Tender Mercies*:

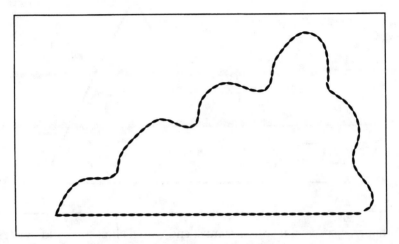

In contrast, some stories are built so that a plot twist suddenly piques the audience's interest, or a slow, peaceful interlude is inserted to give them a breather before the next build begins. For example, here is the roller coaster of an exciting, event-filled horror film with a collection of increasingly terrifying scenes:

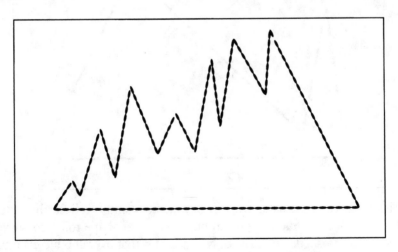

Films as Roller Coasters

Here is the roller coaster of an Agatha Christie–type mystery, with a less emotionally intense series of clues.

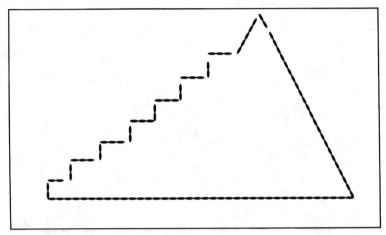

Although a successful structure must end with a climactic build, it doesn't always have to begin slowly. Some films start with a big bang, after which the tensions descend before they begin to rebuild. That kind of structure would be represented by this roller coaster:

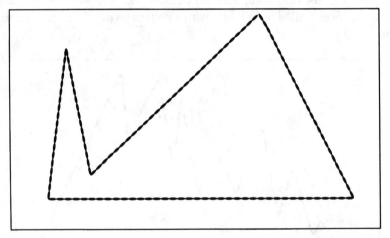

The point is that since the structure of your story simply reflects the patterns of the audience's reactions, you can build whatever shape roller coaster you think will be most effective. The only constant is that overall build eventually must achieve an effective climax and resolution, because it is that big picture pattern that allows the audience to have the satisfaction of real catharsis.

Films as Roller Coasters

The reason for structure's dominance is that the pattern of feelings and sensations largely determines whether the audience will find the experience satisfying or not. Without the compelling experience that occurs when the cumulative pattern of highs and lows creates a successful design, a story can easily become a random collection of interesting moments, too erratic to provide deep emotional satisfaction for the viewers.

II. Plot

Once you have a sense of what kind of roller coaster you want to build, how exactly do you go about it? Often the next step is to develop the *plot*, whose function is to provoke the desired pattern of emotional highs and lows so that viewers will experience the structure as designed. The plot creates the structure by presenting a series of items of information, so an audience reacts with the intended sequence of emotional highs and lows. In this way, the audience's visceral experience matches the pattern you designed.

The height of a story "pillar" reflects the intensity of the audience's emotional reaction to each piece of plot information. For example, if you were dramatizing the following story, you might decide to begin building your roller coaster by giving the audience four key pieces of information:

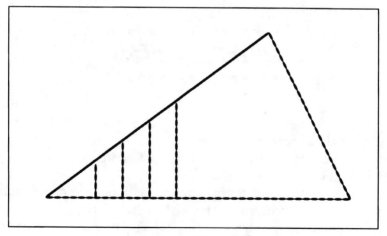

Ascending Story Pillars

In this example, you are building your structure based on the assumption that viewers will care a little bit when they learn that the heroine is a married woman who has just become pregnant, care a little more when they learn that she's already suffered three miscarriages, care more when the doctor says she may have cancer, and care even more when she goes home to her drunken husband who pushes her down the stairs.

The dynamic of story pillars is reminiscent of the game played at state fairs in which people try to force a heavy metal clanger up a vertical pole by hitting the launcher with a sledgehammer. The sensation created in the audience when a pillar "hits the bell" is almost physical. Remember the first time you saw *Body Heat*, for instance? During the final third of the film nearly every scene created that visceral "click" as the emotional stakes pushed higher and higher, and the sensation felt almost like a series of small internal explosions.

Not all stories have to be dramatic, of course; they don't even have to be serious. A story pillar can be built by any kind of emotion—laughter, fear, excitement, or rage. It's the intensity that determines a pillar's height, and it's the height that supports the story's structure. As the story progresses, the pillars must rise higher and higher in order to build to an effective climax and release, but no matter what the pattern is, the overall structure is ultimately supported by the audience's reaction to every individual pillar.

Because of the intricate relationship between plot and structure, many people get them confused. Just remember that your plot is the selection and arrangement of story information; structure is the blueprint of your intended audience reaction to that story information.

III. Characters

Characters are the next major component of a cinematic roller coaster. Their function is to lure your viewers "on board" the ride. After all, it's one thing to watch a roller coaster from a safe distance; it's an entirely different experience actually to get on and take the ride!

Characters fulfill this function by provoking a strong sense of recognition in viewers. Ideally audience members feel as though at least one character is their emotional "proxy," representing some key aspect of their lives. That commonality may be found in the characters' actions, their motives, or in their emotional reactions to events. What's important is that the characters some-how mirror the audience's own experience, for once that bond occurs, the audience feels as though the events of the story were happening to them, thus intensifying the emotional impact of the plot.

IV. Momentum

The next element in constructing a roller coaster is *momentum*, the forward thrust that drives the story through to completion. Momentum is the engine which powers the roller coaster, and its function is to keep the cars moving so that the viewers never have an opportunity to get off. Without momentum, you could design the world's most architecturally impressive roller coaster and even manage to get viewers on board, but without a powerful engine, the cars would just sit there, or slow to a halt at the first dip.

Audiences experience a sense of momentum when they become eager to know the outcome of the story, both how the logical elements will come together and the emotional ramifications of those events. The audience's hunger for information should grow progressively stronger as the story develops, intensifying both the impact of the plot and the emotional connection with characters.

In order to create and focus the audience's eagerness to know what's going to happen next, it's important to give very careful thought to presenting the plot and the characters in a way that provokes the strongest forward thrust. This is often achieved by intentionally planting questions in the viewers' minds—almost like leaving a trail of bread crumbs in a forest, you guide and focus your viewers' attention by the way you give and withhold information, so that they experience a sense of satisfaction when they finally get the "answer" for which they've been searching.

V. Style

The final component of a roller coaster is *style*, whose function is to intensify the key sensations of the ride, those that best convey the essence of your story.

Writers often think of style as an optional decoration that can be applied like a few last-minute curlicues painted on the side of roller-coaster cars. However, it is much more like the difference between riding on a well-greased track that magnifies every twist and turn, or lurching along on a wobbly contraption that feels as if it's going to derail at any moment.

The reason style is so important is that it's virtually omnipresent in the audience's awareness. Long before an audience knows if they like your characters, or if the plot is going to hold their interest, they have a strong and constant sense of the style of the piece, because it's reflected in every line of dialogue or stage description in your script.

Yet because screenwriters are so conscious that they don't have all the stylistic tools available to the maker of a completed film, they often underestimate the profound impact and power of the style choices they have at their disposal, abdicating this area of choice completely, or allowing it to happen at random without regard for which dynamics of the story are being underscored.

The conscious and creative use of concise, well-chosen words can evoke powerful images, sensations, pace, tone, and other atmospheric qualities that can dramatically enhance a script, conveying important aspects of your plot, characters, and momentum, so that the overall ride becomes unified and all-enveloping. However, style functions as an intensifier, so it's important that you use it to enhance the viewers' experience, rather than randomly employing decorative flourishes that can distract from the cohesiveness of the overall ride.

▪ Creating a Great Roller Coaster ▪

Because the elements of a roller coaster can be mixed and matched in almost endless combinations, writers have great variety and freedom in the way they can construct a story roller coaster, as you can see in films like *Room with a View* and *Texas Chainsaw Massacre*. Yet there are some aspects of the story experience which are a constant, so let's discuss those in Chapter Two.

Films as Roller Coasters

QUESTIONS

The more you can begin to recognize each component of a story roller coaster, the more you will identify its contribution to the overall ride. Here are some questions to help you identify these elements in movies you have seen:

1. Which movies have given you the most compelling roller-coaster rides?
2. How would you graph the structure of your three favorite movies?
3. What kinds of roller coasters do you find most exciting as an audience member?
   Are those the same kinds of cinematic roller coasters you try to build?
4. Have you ever gotten "on board" with a compelling character in a movie?
5. Which characters affected you this way?
   What aspect of your hopes or fears did that character represent?
6. Can you think of movies that provoked a strong sense of momentum?
   Can you think of any questions the story made you ask?
7. How does your inner experience differ when there is a strong sense of momentum and when there's not?
8. Which movies have used style effectively for you?
9. Which movies lacked the sense of style they needed?
   Which had so much that it actually distracted from the ride?
10. Which movies have had the best balance of all the above elements?
    What is the connection between that list and the list of your favorite films?

T W O

How Do Roller Coasters Work?

*I*f story roller coasters are so varied, how can there be any constants? What, if anything, do such diverse roller coasters as those for *Police Academy, Psycho, Bringing Up Baby, Friday the Thirteenth,* and *Driving Miss Daisy* have in common?

There are some crucial constants that you must learn to recognize in order to create a compelling roller coaster ride for your audience, but they're not in the external elements of the roller-coaster design. They reside in the internal processes that viewers experience as they ride your roller coaster and try to make sense of both the emotional and logical contents of the story.

These internal audience processes are rarely discussed, perhaps because they are usually experienced at a primal level. But just because the average audience member can't articulate them doesn't mean they aren't important. The truth is that they dominate the audience's subjective experience as they watch your story, so it's crucial that you know how they operate.

Identifying and understanding the mental and emotional needs an audience brings to a story may seem a bit difficult at first because they usually exist on the subconscious level, but they are not irrational or arbitrary, nor unpredictable. Watching yourself watch a film or read a script gives you a chance to become conscious of how audiences react to stories. In fact, as you start to pay attention to your own internal processes when you watch films or read scripts, you will see that they are amazingly consistent and logical, and the more conscious you can become of them, the more clearly you can understand the power of the emotional and intellectual energy you, as a screenwriter, are trying to harness and channel to get viewers involved with your stories.

So let's go back to the beginning, before the formulas, before screenwriting, all the way to the core human dynamics that create the hunger for stories. During most of this book we will be concentrating on techniques of writing for the screen, but before we do that, let's go back to the very foundation of storytelling. Let's find out what an audience wants from a story and why, before we start discussing the "hows" of making successful emotional contact with your viewers.

▪ Back to the Beginning ▪

Mankind has gathered to hear stories since the earliest known societies, but people still haven't had their fill. The storytelling media change with the technologies of each age, but the fundamental urges that drive people to sit at the "story hearth" are as strong today as they were for cave dwellers thousands of years ago. Why do audiences want stories? What sensations do they get? Why are those sensations appealing?

Audiences like stories because stories give them emotional experiences they often can't have in real life. Just as riding a real roller coaster gives people an opportunity to enjoy experiences that are more vivid and exciting than their everyday lives, a captivating story roller coaster provokes the same sense of adventure, excitement, and exhilaration that makes audiences feel truly alive.

Yet most stories are entirely fictional and even those based on fact are still somewhat artificial, so why should a fictionalized story event have such emotional impact on audiences? How can emotions provoked by such an artificial medium be so compelling?

The reason is that people think in stories. Dreams, worries, gossip, religion, myths, and science are all essentially stories that humans have created to give some sense of order, meaning, safety, and security to their lives, which they can't always find in everyday experience. The process of creating stories is so universal that even in the most primitive societies, the inability to string bits of information into a coherent sequence is the definition of "insane," and there are now scientists who speculate that it was this ability, rather than the use of tools, that began to separate humans from other primates.

Yet the mental process of piecing together a jigsaw puzzle, while stimulating to our logical mind, provides a very different sensation from experiencing a satisfying story. In order to be emotionally involving, the pieces of the story eventually have to fit into a whole that is personally meaningful on some level, and the more direct the connection, the more power the story has.

So what kinds of emotional needs do people bring to a story? When we talk about stories being emotionally satisfying, what do we mean?

▪ Getting Away from It All ▪

The entertainment industry has long known that viewers are eager to escape the frustrations of everyday life, so there has been a lot of emphasis on topics and characters that provide fantasy fulfillment. Scores of successful films have offered romanticized versions of viewers' daydreams and vacations from the external frustrations of day-to-day existence.

But there are actually much deeper emotional needs that bring people to the story experience. These come from the desire to find relief from the frustrations that are at the core of the internal human experience. It's the subjective realities of everyday life that actually dominate human experience, and are virtually omnipresent for all people no matter what the external circumstances of their lives. Those needs are grounded in the primal realities that dominate our conscious awareness and our subconscious drives, and an audience's ability to get involved with a story is in direct proportion to how much the story satisfies those needs.

So what are the hungers that propel the audience into your story?

The Four Emotional Needs

There are four core emotional needs an audience brings to any story experience. Since the ultimate emotional success of your script will depend on how well you address these hungers, you must become very conscious of what they are and begin to recognize the connection between those four hungers and the components of a story roller coaster.

1. The Need for New Information

Humans are constantly in a push/pull, love/hate relationship between their desire for new experience and their anxiety about its possible negative consequences. Sometimes referred to as the "neophile/neophobe" conflict (love of the new/fear of the new), most people shuttle back and forth between wanting new stimulation and fearing the consequences every day of their lives.

For example, until a hundred years ago, most people never ventured more than a few miles away from where they were born. Imagine how well they got to know those few miles, and how they must have longed to see what was over the next mountain or beyond the seashore. Yet perhaps they lived in a time when people thought that monsters lurked in the next valley or that the world was flat, so they faced the choice of staying home and safe, or getting answers to questions by risking their lives. Even today, when modern technology has made such physical boundaries less daunting, people are still torn between their desire to engage in new activities and their reluctance to take risks.

Stories are an ideal way to address this hunger. Just as one of the great things about riding a real roller coaster is that it makes passengers feel as though they are hurtling through space uncontrollably while they are actually quite safe, stories let audience members experience fascinating and very frightening new sensations without having to take real-life risks.

Most people's imaginations are filled with hundreds of adventures they'd love to have that simply aren't possible in everyday life. Therefore stories that promise to provide such new sensations attract viewers. *Top Gun* gave audiences a taste of being a fighter pilot, while *The Player* conveyed a sense of what it must feel like to be a Hollywood big shot. Intriguing settings, new sensations, or unknown worlds (whether it's another planet or the behind the scenes glimpse of a more familiar world) promise novelty and therefore enhance a screenplay's appeal by taking viewers into worlds and experiences they may never have on their own.

Satisfying the audience's hunger for new information is often a function fulfilled by the basic idea, but every component of a roller coaster can contain such appeal. Unique characters, unusual momentum devices, and original use of style all have the ability to satisfy the audience's hunger for new stimuli.

2. The Need to Bond

Have you ever taken a wild amusement park ride and gotten stuck sitting with a stranger? At first you may feel uncomfortable, but after you spend a few minutes screaming together or clutching on for dear life, you walk away feeling a real, if temporary, sense of closeness with that person. That's the experience audience members can have if they are able to feel a sense of connection and commonality during a story, either with the characters on the screen or with other members of the audience.

In real life, humans can never really know what others are thinking and feeling, no matter how close they are. In fact, one respected psychologist claims that the majority of people will have only thirteen minutes of genuine intimacy in their entire lives. Only during those few precious minutes of complete emotional bonding will they feel no sense of separation between themselves and others. Thus the hunger to bond is constant and profound, because humans live in an internal world of constant, if unconscious, isolation.

Not only can it be lonely to feel such persistent emotional separation, according to Charles Darwin it can also be dangerous. He believed that animals who were isolated from their social group were more vulnerable, because they had no opportunity to learn which of their emotions to value and act on and which to dismiss. For instance, a young monkey who isn't taught to run away in fear at the sound of a crashing branch may be killed. As a result, Darwin considered a species' ability to synchronize emotions crucial to survival.

That's why people have a great need to have their emotions expressed and affirmed by stories. Watching someone in a story express the same emotions they experience tells people they are not crazy, and that they are not alone. In a story, audiences can also "get inside" characters for long stretches of time, and the more time spent bonded with a character, the more satisfying the story experience will be.

Thus the need for humans to experience emotional bonds, which affirm their inner experience and help them feel connected to the outside world, is a driving, compelling hunger. One of the main reasons people watch films is to satisfy that urge, and if they are successful, the sense of total envelopment helps them achieve catharsis. *Elephant Man* is a film that had that kind of impact on me; students in my class have mentioned *Rocky* or *E.T.* as others that have touched them in that way.

Characters are usually the component of the roller coaster that allows viewers to bond with a story; by exploring characters' thoughts, actions, motives, and dreams, the audience has a chance to recognize the deeper personal truths, even if they've never lived through that specific situation. However, audiences can also bond through plot events that are related to their own lives, momentum devices that pull them into the story, and stylistic elements that make them feel as though they are experiencing the events on the screen firsthand.

3. The Need for Conflict Resolution

Another emotional hunger drawing people to stories is the need to learn more about how to resolve problems, how to deal with conflict and change, and how to take appropriate action. Many people avoid these in real life due to the possible negative consequences, so they live in a constant state of internal vigilance against their own emotions of anger or resentment of injustice. Yet it takes a great deal of energy to constantly hold in emotions, so people develop a strong need to "act" vicariously on such conflicts as a way of venting the emotional pressure inside their own heads.

A real roller coaster provides riders with a sense of "triumph" at the end for surviving each exciting twist and turn, even though they were really just passive observers. Story roller coasters offer a similar sensation—the audience can vicariously explore what it's like to act in confrontations and face grave danger without paying the price.

Audiences like stories that help them understand how to face and triumph over conflict, whether it's physical as in *K2* or emotional as in *The Accidental Tourist*. The element of stories which deals with this is the plot, providing an opportunity to handle change and conflict vicariously, providing role models, warnings, lessons, and encouragement that can help viewers deal with their everyday lives. However, conflict resolution can also be addressed in provocative characterizations, momentum devices that make audiences struggle to put together the pieces of the puzzle, and stylistic elements that intensify the sense of danger and risk.

4. The Need for Completion

The last great need for which people come to stories derives from the fact that humans are forced to live their entire lives lacking full knowledge about almost everything, yet they must make decisions and take action every day. The constant effort to act despite incomplete information is, at the least, very tiring and sometimes profoundly disturbing. Consequently, one of the strongest desires people have is to take a vacation from the gnawing sense of uncertainty, and spend time in a world where they are confident that issues will be resolved and all questions will be answered.

That's why stories that convey the promise of completion and order are the most satisfying, because these are exactly the sensations that people can't usually find in real life. When they ride a real roller coaster, they may feel as though they are experiencing random twists and turns, but despite the sensation of unpredictability, they know that the cars will eventually roll to a halt, the ride will be over, and they will be able to look back on the experience as finite and complete. Story roller coasters constructed to give riders the confidence that "all will be revealed" also have a tremendous appeal which has as much to do with the way a story is told as the topic itself.

Viewers are willing to undergo extended periods of suspense and mystery as long as the questions are answered by the end. For example, "Twin Peaks" was a fabulous experiment in television. Its style, sensibility, characterizations, and world view were absolutely captivating. It was only in the area of promising completion that it eventually failed, yet that was enough to drive viewers away once they lost faith that their most central questions would be answered.

Momentum is the aspect of a story that promises the audience completion by providing a satisfying pattern of mental "questions and answers" which viewers experience as they move through a story. However, the sense of completion can also be conveyed in plots that make logical sense, character arcs that seem complete and convincing, and stylistic choices that intensify the key moments of discovery as the viewers put together the pieces of the story puzzle.

The Five Mental Processes

Even though viewers are hungry to have their emotional needs met, the analytical nature of the human brain can distract them from becoming emotionally absorbed unless your story makes logical sense. Therefore, in addition to the four emotional hungers, you also need to understand the five mental processes through which an audience makes sense out of any story.

1. Resistance

Often writers assume that the audience is totally open to the storytelling experience simply because they have have purchased tickets or turned on the TV. However, the viewers actually experience a strong sense of initial resistance that you need to understand in order to overcome it.

To understand this resistance, imagine sitting in a room where a movie screen suddenly drops down and the lights begin to dim. Wouldn't you feel an immediate sense of tension? "Will this be boring?" "Will I enjoy it?" "Will I be able to get out if I want to leave?" The more cinematically literate our society becomes, the harder it is to get audiences to open up and give themselves completely to the storytelling experience. Too many times, movies that are supposed to be great turn out to be duds, and the new hit television shows are a bore.

One way Hollywood has tried to solve this is by encouraging writers to create big openings in the first ten pages. There should be something compelling to capture the audience's attention, but a big action scene isn't the only way to do it. Once you understand the dynamic you are trying to create, you can choose from hundreds of ways to get the audience involved in your story. You can lure them, charm them, shock them, amuse them, make them curious, or create practically any other compelling emotion, as long as it works within the overall unity of your story.

2. Need for Orientation

As viewers try to make sense of your story, their minds start looking for landmarks that they can use to orient themselves. "Who is that character?" "Why are they in this building?" "What are they doing?" Viewers' minds are searching for clues, so, in that sense, every story is a mystery, no matter what its genre.

Therefore, storytelling styles that give clear emphasis to key information help minimize confusion and distraction. The faster viewers can figure out what and who is important, the sooner they can begin to understand the emotional significance of events, which is what allows their own subjective roller-coaster experience to begin to climb.

3. Expanding from Landmarks

Once viewers begin to feel oriented, they start to build on that knowledge based on which pieces of new information seem pertinent to what they've already decided is important. Each piece of information they think is important becomes a dot, then they try to connect the dots and tell the best possible story from the available information.

Thus you must make very sure that you are aware of what the key information is, and that you clearly convey it to your viewers, so that they are constructing the same overview of your story as the one you intend them to experience.

4. Assessing the Effort

If viewers are able to assemble the pieces quickly and easily, they feel encouraged to become more emotionally involved; if the pieces are hard to put together, the effort involved can really drag down an audience's enthusiasm for the story.

Recent studies of people responding to music indicate that the ease with which audiences can create a meaningful pattern out of a melodic Strauss waltz is a major source of their enjoyment; however, making sense out of dissonant, progressive jazz is much harder, and many people will eventually withdraw from the experience because the pleasure they are deriving isn't worth the effort it takes.

The same is true for people's involvement in a story. If the ratio between an audience's moment-to-moment efforts and the moment-to-moment satisfaction becomes too lopsided, the audience will start to lose interest because their conscious awareness of their unrequited efforts makes them feel vulnerable in a manner which most viewers don't like. If obtaining the information becomes too difficult, or if too much useless information is obtained, viewers will eventually feel alienated from the story.

5. Continuous Process of Decisions

Often writers make the mistake that the audience's assessment of whether the story experience was worthwhile only comes at the end of the story. However, studies have shown that the audience is actually in a constant process of making decisions, which is what is reflected in the moment-to-moment ups and downs seen in the structure. As a result, even if you are building a roller coaster that peaks to one major and compelling moment at the end, you must still tell your story in a way that holds the viewers' interest and emotional involvement from the first moment to the last.

Minimizing the Negative Space

All these emotional and mental processes take place in the viewers' *"negative space,"* the part of their minds not completely absorbed by the story.

In Asian art, there are two kinds of energy in any painting. One is the "positive space," which is filled with the visible decoration; the "negative space" is the portion that is empty, or at least that's how it looks to Westerners' eyes. However, the whole point of the positive/negative approach to art is that there really is no empty space; both aspects of the painting are crucial, and the proportion between them ultimately determines whether the artwork is effective.

The same is true for an audience's experience of a story. The positive space is the information conveyed in the story; the negative space is the viewers' subjective thoughts, efforts, focus, energy, and concentration as they attempt to process the information coming from the positive space in your story. If processing the information takes too much effort, their awareness remains dominated by the negative space, and that distances viewers from your story. However, if the process of making sense out of a story is not too difficult, their focus will eventually shift to the positive space, allowing their negative space to recede. This shift allows the positive space to dominate their consciousness, which in turn enables them to become increasingly involved in your story.

Thus the goal for a dramatist is to maximize the emotional appeal of the positive space so much that viewers allow the negative space to fade away, at least for a little while. When both the intellectual and emotional needs are met, audiences are able to give themselves completely to the experience of the story.

Just because the audience has these needs doesn't mean that you must address them immediately; exciting sensations can be created for the audience when those hungers are postponed in an intriguing and tantalizing way. But your chances of meeting those needs decrease sharply if you're not even conscious that they exist. That's why understanding these core emotional and logical processes is so crucial.

The conventional rules of storytelling have evolved from efforts to meet these audience hungers, and often some have proven successful over time. However, the more writers use those now-familiar solutions, the more cliché and ineffectual they become. So one of the major challenges of being a successful storyteller is to find new ways to meet those age-old needs.

How Do Roller Coasters Work?

So what's a writer to do? The way to write a great screenplay is to find the solutions that best fit the needs of your roller coaster, because every choice you make in your screenplay will either enhance or detract from your audience's ability to become absorbed in your story's positive space. The secret is not to rely on old conventional wisdom and rules, but really to understand the relationship between the "whys" and "hows" so that you will feel free to break with convention whenever you need to make other choices to bring your cinematic roller coaster to life.

Now that you have a sense of what an audience's process is, in Chapter Three let's talk about the intellectual and emotional challenges of your own that you must face during the creative process.

QUESTIONS

As we go through this book, you will see again and again that it is these same story dynamics that are at the core of every aspect of storytelling, so the more viscerally you are aware of your own internal processes, the more you can understand exactly what emotional and intellectual reactions you are trying to provoke from your audience.

Think about the last time you saw a movie:

1. What did you feel when the movie began?
   When did you feel the first sense of excitement?
2. What questions did you find yourself asking?
   How easy was it for you to find the answers?
   What reactions did you have if the movie answered them effectively?
   What reactions did you have if it didn't?
3. If you ultimately decided the film was bad,
   When did you realize it?
   What made you first suspect? Why?
   When were you sure?
   How did you feel when you reached your conclusion?
4. What happened if you thought the film was good?
5. What kinds of activities were going on in your negative space?
   Were they enhancing your enjoyment of the movie, or were they distracting?
6. When you got bored, how dominant did your negative space become?
   When you were really involved, how dominant was it?
7. Were you more aware of the positive space or the negative as the movie progressed?
   How did that correlate with your overall enjoyment of the film?
8. Which was the strongest attraction in the film for you?
   New stimulation?
   Bonding?
   Conflict resolution?
   Promise of completeness?
9. What films are your favorites?
   What lured you onto those roller coasters?
   Which of the four hungers did the story most appeal to?
10. Have you ever felt total catharsis in a film?
    How many of the hungers did that film fulfill for you?

THREE

Creativity: The Building Process

I used to think that the hardest part of the creative process was dealing with the tough outside world. But the more writers I meet, the more I realize that the biggest obstacle is often the internal sense of confusion, indecision, and doubt that can plague the creative mind during actual writing. Therefore, before we continue discussing the aspects of a successful story roller coaster, let's examine the core creative process. Writers who find a dependable approach for dealing with creative challenges usually are able to continue writing long enough to become at least a modest success, while those who never master a method of overcoming such problems usually end up dropping out and never achieving their dreams.

Psychologists warn about the power of an unconscious belief; just because impulses aren't conscious doesn't mean they're not dominating your thinking, and I think this is particularly true for the creative process. In fact, the more unconscious the impulses are, the more they can control you, because you don't have a chance to use your logic or conscious willpower to counteract them. You need to bring the entire process up to the conscious level, which will dramatically increase your chances of finding the approach to screenwriting that works best for you.

So before we look at the technique of building a screenplay, let's look at the process of being creative. It's an area that's rarely examined in depth, yet almost every problem encountered in screenwriting ultimately stems from a misunderstanding of its basic challenges.

The Creative Process

By its very nature, the creative process is an attempt to take intangible, often highly subjective ideas, emotions, and sensations and express them to the outside world. In fact, the core of the creative drive is the hunger to express the world as the writer sees it, which means first getting in touch with those inner truths. Some of these internal messages may be easy to access and unintimidating to express. For example, it's usually not too scary to tell the world your thoughts on politics or the type of music you like. But the core of such opinions often lies much deeper.

The human brain makes associations between various ideas and/or objects, and there are many socially acceptable ways to "connect the dots." But humans also make subjective, even irrational, connections based on their experiences, personalities, and observations. These are the connections that the world may not understand or even approve of, and so people try to keep them hidden away, perhaps even from themselves. Yet those same distinctive connections are the source of a writer's most personal truths and powerful emotions.

Things can become confusing at this stage because writers are often torn between two strong polarities—the need to express themselves and the desire to avoid whatever psychological pain may be involved. Even if the topic is a lighthearted comic romp, not scary on a conscious level, revealing the mind's inner logic still feels risky. Hence the mind can create very effective defense mechanisms, greatly complicating a seemingly simple series of creative choices.

Since a writer's goal during the creative process is to dredge up very private material and make it not only conscious but *public*, writers often get stuck in a tug-of-war between the side of them that wants expression and acceptance, and the side that wants to hide. The two halves battle back and forth, and anyone who's ever gone through it knows how overwhelming the internal struggle can be. The core challenge of the creative process is to deal with the internal push/pull without losing clarity and focus, because the same search for inner truths that can shut writers down can also make their writing come alive.

I wish I could tell you that there is a simple, easy way to avoid this messy part of screenwriting, but the truth is that the creative process is messy—damn messy—and there are very few writers I know who go through a story without some moments of feeling lost or confused. However, understanding how the creative process works can take away some of the fear and help you find an approach that will allow you to go deep into those dark interior woods confident that you can find your way out again.

The Creative Challenge

The initial phase of writing is usually a thrill. You get an idea that really speaks to you, and for a while you're certain you can capture all its wonderful nuances and excitement, so you start off, confident and happy.

Then you hit a wall. Sometimes you're facing a major creative problem, sometimes it's only a minor concern, but your inability to find a satisfactory solution makes you doubt yourself. If the situation continues, that doubt can evolve into fear—fear that you can't do justice to the idea, or even fear that the idea isn't worth doing justice to. You may try to fight the fear by ignoring it, plowing past uncertainties, and arguing with that nagging voice in your head, because you're determined not to get stuck. Yet that reaction rarely resolves the initial creative dilemma.

The worse the inner confusion becomes, the more appealing screenwriting formulas may seem, and often you may start changing the core of your idea in order to fit some predetermined mold. You begin denying your instincts and working more from your head, but the emotional center of your story shifts increasingly as you get further from your original vision. Standardized rules and formulas rarely fit your story exactly, and you become plagued further by doubts. "What am I doing wrong? Why can't I figure this out? How can I be a good writer if these rules don't feel right to me?"

Some writers force themselves to trudge forward; others abandon any conscious use of craft, determined not to compromise the integrity of their story. Initially the rejection of craft can seem very freeing, but ultimately it works no better than the formulaic approach. Depending only on instinctive choices often results in decisions that seem right one day and wrong the next; you make changes and more changes, but it seems that you're just making your story different instead of better.

At this point the "pinball effect" begins. You start shuttling back and forth between allegiance to rules and disdain for formula, losing sight of your original vision and getting bored by the familiarity of the choices formulas encourage you to make. The longer the confusion goes on, the more distracting it becomes, forcing you to focus your creative energy on which approach you should use rather than on your screenplay.

▪ Craft vs. Creativity ▪

The hidden premise of such either/or thinking is that craft and creativity are mutually exclusive and innately adversarial. There are writers, and successful ones, who use one or the other, and not only swear by their choice but are passionately convinced that the other way leads to rack and ruin.

Yet writers who abandon their instincts and writers who refuse to use craft are both making the same mistake. Using only one or the other is like trying to cross the ocean guided only by intuition, or staying in a cabin using only instruments and maps. To increase your chance of a safe crossing you need both, using one to double-check the other, because they allow you to have the widest possible range of options to overcome any challenge that occurs.

The reason you need craft and creativity is that each serves a different function, and like the left-brain, right-brain interaction of the human mind, both have a vital place in the creative process. A great script needs the spark of creative passion and excitement that only inspiration can provide, as well as the clarity and logic that only command of craft can ensure, since a successful screenplay must orchestrate both the intellectual and emotional energies of the audience.

The right brain helps you develop an instinctive sense of what you want your story to accomplish, while the left brain helps determine what tools of the craft will best achieve that goal. Like an architect who must have a solid command of craft but whose success will come from the ability to use it imaginatively, being a good screenwriter means that you must find the right longitude and latitude between your brain and your heart. You must dominate the tools and fundamentals of your craft, but ultimately your selection of how and why to use them should transcend simplistic formulas and rules and be inspired by your own, more personal, and more exciting world view.

What do I mean when I talk about a world view? I mean the writer's individual take on things, the specific angle from which the writer views life. The more you make contact with those personal insights, the more vivid and original your writing can be. For example, let's say you're writing about a mother who is very frightening to her child. Through your right-brain creativity, you remember a powerful image from your childhood of your mother wearing bright red shoes. Since that image immediately provokes in you exactly the kind of emotions you want your audience to have, you might decide to include that scene exactly as you see it in your mind.

However, since the audience wasn't raised by your mother, chances are that the image of red shoes will not provoke in them exactly the same kinds of feelings as yours—unless you make sure that the audience has enough clues to translate the image. To make sure they understand, you might add dialogue, descriptive mood music, or whatever you think is necessary to make its importance clear.

The awareness that you must help the audience make those desired associations is the beginning of the respect for craft; the ability to have original, imaginative, and inventive images to translate demands access to creativity. After reading literally thousands of scripts, I can tell you that the best scripts are those in which both craft and creativity are working at the highest level.

▪ Asking the Right Questions ▪

The way to make sure that you have access to both is to incorporate craft and creativity into the very core of your writing approach. In many ways, the creative process is just a series of asking and answering questions, so in order to have the best possible chance to solve the creative challenges, you must ask the questions that allow your mind to search through both creativity and craft for the best possible solutions.

The problem with most formulaic approaches is that they encourage you to go about writing in the opposite way. By telling you what the contents should be, or in what order the events must occur, it is as if they are telling you the answers, which, in turn, forces your creative energy to ask only questions that will produce those specific results. Almost like the "Jeopardy" game show, by controlling what questions you ask, formulas control your entire creative process.

Emotionally that may feel helpful at first because it minimizes some initial confusion, but if you lose control of what questions you will answer, you have lost control of your story and your script. That's why you can feel so lost, and also the reason your screenplay focus blurs—it's because step by step you have begun aiming your creativity at the wrong target.

However, if you ask yourself "function" questions, which focus your creative energies on the story function you are trying to fulfill rather than just solving isolated story dilemmas, let your imagination roam until it finds the right answer. You can have the best of both worlds by using the clarity of craft while retaining the freedom of creativity. Having access to both aspects of the creative process allows you to set up a bridge between the left and right sides of your mind; you can then move back and forth whenever you need to, focusing on craft if you feel yourself getting lost and on creativity if your solutions seem too pat. That shuttle is the central active element in the creative experience. That process allows your mind to scan from horizon to horizon to seek out your best solutions.

Understanding the function that each element of the roller coaster fulfills is crucial, because it allows you to start forming function questions. Yet in addition to mastering the craft of writing, it's crucial that you learn to hear, and trust, your own instincts, because understanding both gives you the best chance of finding the ideal intersection of heart and head.

▪ An Educated Gut ▪

The *educated gut* is where the intellectual and emotional meet. When you have an "educated gut," it means that you receive visceral signals from your creative instincts, yet have enough command of craft to translate their message with clarity and confidence. When the creative process is not approached with clear internal signals, it can be terrifying to writers, because they associate its search mode with feeling lost and losing control. However, the real problem is not that their minds are searching for answers, but that they are not recognizing the right answer if and when they find it.

Many writers are scared to trust their instincts. Yet it has been my experience that people who care enough to devote time, money, and energy to mastering the creative process usually have a very strong and very accurate internal guidance system—if they will only listen to it! Most of the time when I give notes in script sessions, the writers already know what I'm talking about. They've sensed the problem too, but they didn't listen to their instincts because those impulses were contrary to existing formulas or because they pointed out problems the writers didn't know how to solve.

In fact, I have rarely known a writer's gut to be entirely wrong if it's responding to a basic "yes or no" question about "Is this choice working?" The problem occurs when writers confuse their gut instincts for the answer to "What technique should I use?" The reason is that instinct is not usually a reliable source for selecting craft, which demands a more rational, conscious, left-brain consideration of possible alternatives, making sure all bases are covered.

But even the best gut in the world is no good unless you can understand its messages. You must recognize that click that happens inside you when something really sparks. Without that recognition of the sensation that tells you you've stumbled onto the right solution, you will never experience the deepest and most fulfilling satisfaction of writing.

Additionally, without that click, you can't "hear" the audience's needs and hungers, because you won't recognize your own. Finally, such access to the full scope of your imagination is the best way to find your unique voice as a writer.

Once you learn to recognize the click of creative satisfaction that occurs when you've found an answer that works, you can then feel freer to explore the outer reaches of both your craft and creativity, because you will feel confident that you can find your way home again. That's when writing becomes really fun, when you feel confident enough to make up your own rules and techniques, ones that really sparkle with excitement and are truest to the individual project you are working on. The reason you need access to your impulses and instincts is that the more you listen to your imagination, the more freely and readily it will function.

Honor Your Impulses

Listening to your instincts about what feels right and what feels wrong is an indispensable step in becoming the best possible writer. Many writers, however, become so convinced that there is one right way to write a screenplay that they assume any internal signals to the contrary are the result of laziness, weakness, lack of discipline, or lack of talent. As a result, every time they have such an impulse, they ignore it, or decide it must be retrained, cutting themselves off from the deepest source of their talent at the roots.

Just as in psychology, where patients emotionally shut down every time they start judging themselves as bad or inadequate, every time you tell yourself "If I were a really good writer, I wouldn't have this problem," you stop your creative juices from flowing. What you need to do instead is learn to recognize your instincts and accept them as a constant, and important, part of the creative process.

Try different approaches. Experiment. Keep what works, and toss out what doesn't. There is no right way to write, only a way that works for you. Just as painters have a much better chance of producing exciting, original, and successful work once they recognize that they prefer to work with charcoal or oils, you must find the times, the locations, the processes that work best for you. The following chapters are offered only as a way to jog your own creative energies, because nothing will ever be more valuable in writing a great screenplay than being in touch with your own creative process.

QUESTIONS

1. Have you used screenwriting formulas before?
  How did they work for you?
  Did they make you feel safe and comfortable?
  Did they make you feel confined and trapped?
  Were you pleased with the end result?
  Were you comfortable with the process?

2. Which aspect is easier for you—craft or creativity?

3. Which is a stronger drive for you—self-expression or fear of exposure?

4. How much do you trust yourself as a writer?

5. What do you think your weaknesses are?
  What are your strengths?

6. Which phase of the writing process comes easiest to you?
  The beginning? The middle? The end?

7. Which part makes you most nervous?
  Why?

8. Next time you write a screenplay, do you have any thoughts about what you'd like to do differently?

9. How often do you second-guess your own instincts?

10. When you get back comments on your own writing, how often do they address the same concerns you already had?

11. Can you tell when you've found a solution that feels right?

12. What do your own gut sensations feel like?
  How easy is it for you to translate these sensations?

FOUR

The Most Valuable Tool You Have

Now that you understand both the audience's needs and your own internal process, how do you select an idea that is rich enough to satisfy both?

I believe that if there is something about an idea that genuinely excites you, there is a way to tell that story so that others can feel the same excitement. But in order to do that, you need to find out *exactly* what it is about the idea that excites you. What about the idea captures your imagination? Why does it seem important to you? Why do you want to tell that story?

The Dramatic Center

The greatest tool that you as a writer have is that visceral click, that sudden jolt, that spasm of excitement that makes you jump up in the middle of the night and grab a pencil, or "sshh" everyone in earshot so that you can hear the rest of a news item on the TV, or rip out an article while reading a magazine in your doctor's waiting room. Of all the creative impulses that a writer can feel, this one is the most compelling, because it's the moment an idea with real personal power has suddenly bubbled up from your subconscious, and its message is freshest in your mind.

I call the idea that provokes the special combination of inspiration and physical sensation the *dramatic center*, and it signals the exact epicenter of your creative excitement about an idea. The dramatic center is supremely valuable for several reasons. It clarifies just what it is about the idea that seems so important to you. It also allows you to know what emotions you want to elicit in your viewers. You want the audience to have an experience that leads them to feel the way you do about your story.

Another reason it's so valuable is that many writers find it difficult to penetrate or reveal their deepest emotional concerns. An idea that has a powerful hold on the individual can sometimes be hard for a writer to gain access to through rational thinking because of subconscious resistance. But at that exact moment of eruption, the very power that makes an idea explode up to your conscious level signals the presence of a deeply held personal truth.

The moment of discovery is usually accompanied by a visceral sensation. For me it's a sudden intake of breath and tightening at the top of my back; for you, it might be a rush of adrenaline or a clutching feeling in your chest. No matter what its form, its usefulness comes from the fact that its unmistakable physical signal means you can always locate it in your body, allowing you to return to the core of your inspiration whenever you begin to feel lost. The physical sensation that accompanies a dramatic center can function almost like the beep-beep-beep of a Geiger counter, guiding you back to that core whenever you feel you may be drifting away. As a result, you will have a compass that can be your infallible guide through all the difficult hours of soul searching and decision making it takes to write a good script.

To illustrate the power of the dramatic center, let's say you were hired to write an updated version of *Othello*. At first glance, it's easy to see that the play's theme is jealousy, and you could always start generating your approach to the material from that kind of intellectual observation. But I can guarantee that your script will be much more explosive once you are really in touch with what jealousy means to you. How do you feel about feeling jealous? Proud? Ashamed? Possessive? Exhilarated? What exactly makes you jealous and why? Suddenly you are drawing from a much richer, more stimulating pool of images and associations, one that allows the audience to glimpse the world through your eyes—giving them the taste of new information, which makes a story so exciting.

Look what Peter Shaffer did when he was writing *Amadeus*. It would have been easy to write a straightforward, chronological approach to Mozart's life; other writers might have been intrigued by Mozart's poverty, or the majesty of the musician's creative genius. However, Shaffer was fascinated with the terror of being mediocre, and that's what he wrote about in *Amadeus*. It is his uniquely personal insight that makes his script so compelling. Not every writer has Shaffer's command of craft. But writers will always deliver their best material when they are working from a stance of passion and commitment.

A clear dramatic center helps your motivation as well. Discovering the dramatic center of an idea allows you to develop a personalized passion about the topic, which unlocks an astonishing cache of power and dedication. The more conscious you become of the power of your own personal truth, the more determined you will be to express it.

Discovering the Dramatic Center

I discovered both the existence and the power of a genuine dramatic center when I was running a small theater in Washington, D.C. I had always been intrigued by the story of Lizzie Borden, the infamous nineteenth-century woman honored in the doggerel:

> Lizzie Borden took an ax
> And gave her mother forty whacks;
> When she saw what she had done
> She gave her father forty-one!

So I announced in the fall that the last show of our spring season would be a play that I would write about Lizzie.

Now, I had always known that I was fascinated by Lizzie Borden. She was a thirty-two-year-old spinster accused of killing her father and her stepmother in 1892. She lived in a small New England town that valued propriety above all else, and Lizzie seemed to be the perfect New England spinster. She never showed her feelings in public, never criticized her family, and never spoke about her own desires. Her family was connected to one of the wealthiest families in the area, but her own father was a penny-pincher who forced the family to live in a rundown part of town, made them eat rotting mutton stew, and was generally a withdrawn and controlling man.

I spent three weeks in Fall River, Massachusetts, and by the end felt confident that I knew everything about the case. I had found a myriad of fascinating details, bits of real dialogue, and other insights that I was certain would add power and authenticity to the play.

So I began writing my script. I wrote and wrote and wrote, and threw scenes away, and wrote some more. I tried various approaches starting on the morning of the murder, beginning with the trial and doing flashbacks, and any other combination I could think of. Eventually I had written at least three of what I now refer to as "rotten mutton" drafts, in which I tried to cleverly arrange and rearrange the details of the real chronological story. Unfortunately, each version was worse than the one before.

Meanwhile, the clock was ticking. I had publicly committed my theater to a play on Lizzie Borden, and the more lost I got, the more desperate I got. I had to find out what was wrong with my script!

Then one night, when I was pacing the floor trying to figure out what to try next, I started asking myself again and again why I had wanted to write the play in the first place, and suddenly realized that I identified with Lizzie Borden! I didn't consciously understand why, but I immediately recognized the truth of the visceral thunderbolt. As I kept exploring, my entire body began to feel constricted, and eventually I realized that, for me, Lizzie was a symbol of repression. Although I had been born a hundred years later and raised in a seemingly different world, I saw in her story the same anger and frustration that I had felt trying (unsuccessfully) to be a proper Southern belle.

Once I understood that repression was the dramatic center of my story, I understood why all of the "rotten mutton" drafts had been so ineffective. I had been making creative choices almost at random, blindly following conventional formats simply because I didn't know what I was trying to say. Once I understood that the play was about repression, everything suddenly became clear.

My first realization was that my story roller coaster had to be designed in such a way that the audience would experience the same relentless sense of constriction and confinement that I felt was crucial to understanding Lizzie. My earlier dramatizations of Lizzie had focused on various grisly aspects of her personal life, thus creating a roller coaster of this pattern:

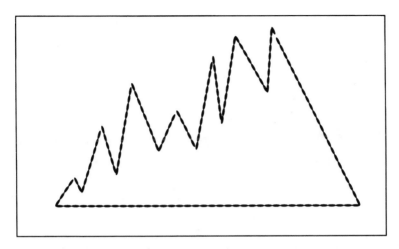

However, now that I knew I didn't want the audience to have an opportunity for venting their sense of frustration, I knew I had to build the kind of roller coaster that didn't allow audience emotions to erupt. I had to create an emotional experience for them that made them as hungry for that final explosion as Lizzie was, if only to release their pent-up frustrations.

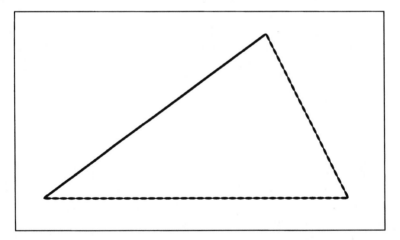

Once I had a clear sense of the structure I was trying to build, the next level of decision making concerned the plot and characters. Eventually I changed the piece from a portrayal of Lizzie's actual life into a broader piece in which Lizzie was only one of four period women suffering terribly from deep internal trauma but not allowed to express themselves because of societal expectation.

The Most Valuable Tool You Have

At the beginning of the play they seemed like characters from *Little Women*; by the end, the audience realized that three of the women were well mannered but completely insane; one woman had never accepted the death of her fiancé years ago, one had never gotten over the sudden loss of a child, and one pretended to love her sickly elder sister, while actually letting the woman starve to death during the course of the play. Only Lizzie refused to ignore her own emotions, and only Lizzie had any chance of breaking out of her confines. Unfortunately, with no healthy role models for conflict resolution, her solution was ghastly, but when the play ended (just before the murders) the audience almost cheered! Their response wasn't because they approved of her morality, but because they had developed their own deep need to vent the sense of confinement and restriction they had experienced during the course of the play.

Clarity on my dramatic center also helped me understand exactly what questions I wanted the audience to be thinking about as they watched the play, and how to use stylistic elements to enhance the audience's sense of confinement and restriction. It showed me how to use dialogue to intensify the characters' sense of isolation, how to use colors to express the monotony of such a limited way of life, what textures would best convey the rigidity of that world, and even what kind of music I wanted to use. I'm not saying that every audience member consciously understood that the play was about repression. However, the version I finally staged was quite successful, because once I knew the epicenter of the idea, I had both the inspiration and clarity to make exciting and unified choices throughout the play, allowing me to send the same unified message to the audience on both the conscious and subconscious level.

That's why I'm such a big believer in the dramatic center. It provides you with a crystal-clear understanding of the unifying dynamic of your story, allowing all the components to merge into one cohesive whole. Unfortunately, most writers don't feel the need to be so specific about what intrigues them about an idea. They often assume that if they feel drawn to a topic, the reasons are self-evident, or contained within the external elements of the idea. However, the real creative power of your topic lies not in external packaging, but in your internal associations with the idea. Often it's not the events, but the interpretation that is riveting. When writers begin to use story material as a Rorschach test to reflect the issues that are important to them, suddenly the same basic topic begins to come to life.

Dramatic Center vs. Theme

When I talk about the dramatic center in my classes, I am often asked about the difference between the dramatic center and a *theme*. From the point of view of the audience, the two terms may seem very much the same. In fact, if you asked audience members to express what emotional message they got from your story, their attempts to articulate their emotional realization might sound very much like a theme.

However, a dramatic center is a visceral sensation that is an internal tool for the writer. One quick way to define it is how you, the writer, *feel* about the theme. As experienced from the point of view of the writer, theme is analytical and objective, while a dramatic center is emotional and subjective. Theme is a conscious statement of intent, an intellectualized observation of impersonal assumptions, while a dramatic center is an impassioned insight into your personal values. The advantage of using a theme as the focus of your creative efforts is that it is often easier to access, since it is both external and conscious. But an intellectualized idea doesn't give out the clear beep-beep-beep of a internal Geiger counter; it simply doesn't have the same emotional power.

Finding that internal Geiger counter is so valuable because once you've found it, its visceral signals can be located again no matter how tired or discouraged or confused you get. We all know how easy it is to get lost in the writing process; one day you're confident that you're on the right track, and the next you're in the darkest despair. An idea that you are only committed to in your head can quickly become gibberish. The more you think, the more you second-guess yourself, and soon you're reacting to reactions. Like making copies of copies, suddenly you're generations away from your original clarity and inspiration.

• Finding Your Dramatic Center •

Each idea you have contains its own dramatic center, but in order to have access to its full power, you must locate and identify it exactly.

The way it usually happens for me is that I'll be reading an article or some other research material on an idea that I'm already interested in when suddenly I'll feel that jolt that I've come to know and value so well. I immediately stop what I'm doing, and give all of my attention to memorizing the physical sensation while it's still fresh in my body. I then try to find a word, an image, or sound that I can then use as a reminder to help me find it again whenever I need to regain clarity. I then test it, to make sure that the image or phrase provokes the same reaction each time I think about it. With Lizzie, I eventually found a piece of music that did the trick; with a screenplay I was going to direct, it was a mental photograph. Every time I summoned it into my consciousness, I felt the same thunderbolt of compassion that was my dramatic center for that project.

One of the ways I know I've found the real dramatic center of my idea is that I feel a visceral click, a compelling mix of relief, clarity, certainty, and excitement. Another way is that my mind begins to act like a magnet for images, music, ideas that I may not have thought about for years. Suddenly I remember a painting I used to love, or a piece of music that once touched me deeply. The old saw "Nothing is wasted on a writer" suddenly seems amazingly true. Within minutes, concepts and images that may have been floating around in my mind suddenly make sense, and I can see how the dramatic center expresses the connection between them.

The important thing to remember is that you're not looking for an intellectualized idea, but a sensation, a jolt of excitement that is strong enough to be recognized whenever you need to find it again. It's also important to make sure that you write it down. You think you'll remember it, but you won't. The very fact that it's a momentary breakthrough from your subconscious almost guarantees that your defense mechanism will swallow it up again as soon as it gets a chance. So make sure that you've jotted down the idea or image, so that you can come back to it later and find it again.

Ideally, you should try to identify your dramatic center before you ever write a line, but often that's not possible. It's good to start looking for it as soon as possible in that it's often easier to locate before you get locked into preconceptions of your material. Even when it's not coming easily, you should never really give up. If you wonder whether you've found it or not, you probably haven't, because the sense of confidence and clarity you instinctively feel once you've found your "compass" is unmistakable.

Sometimes the dramatic center comes first, and as you explore the sensation, you discover what your story should be. Sometimes it happens the other way around—you've discovered an idea you'd love to write about but can't figure out exactly what the dramatic center is. If you are able to find your compass early, it will help you ensure that the many layers of your story all express the same world view.

The Most Valuable Tool You Have

One way to encourage the emergence of the dramatic center of an idea that intrigues you is simply to be honest. Hemingway once said, "Write the truest sentence you know," and I think that's particularly true for finding the dramatic center of your idea. The dramatic center is such a deep expression of who you are and what you believe, that anything less than your deepest truth is unlikely to reveal it. For a writer, a story is the way to tell the truth. You must believe in what your story says, which means that you have to get deep-down honest. In that sense, *every* story is a personal confession.

That is not to say that all writing should be autobiographical. In fact, many writers become blocked when they try to create a literal presentation of their own lives; they have not yet become aware of why a certain incident was so important to them, so they can't present it to others with clarity. But even when you're writing something that seems to be entirely fictional, if the idea really "calls" to you, there is something in the idea that really touches your core.

The advice "write what you know" may help you to discover your dramatic center, but it also can be misleading, because too many people think that it means you must write about only the events that have actually happened to you. "What you know" can also include those topics that you are really drawn to, those topics that set your imagination swirling, whether or not you have actually experienced them. In fact, even if your goal is to write the world's greatest genre piece, you need to find some way to transcend the audience's expectations, and you simply can't do that without gaining access to your own imagination, creativity, and insights. It is exactly the insights that arise during your soul searching that makes writing exciting. My friend, writer Oliver Hailey, used to say that he loved to write because he loved to find out what he thought about things!

Another way to discover the dramatic center of your idea is to develop a profile of yourself as artist. Ask yourself what type of stories historically have caught your attention. Are there places or times in the past that you feel passionate about? Are current social issues or personalities intriguing to you? The reason this process can be helpful is that since your dramatic center is a statement of personal truths, there are often similarities between the dramatic centers of various pieces. It is often easier to get objectivity on a piece that you have already written, or haven't begun yet, because your creative ego doesn't have so much at stake. Therefore, once you are able to locate the dramatic center in any of your works or ideas, it may be a good clue to finding it in your current piece.

The Most Valuable Tool You Have

It can also be helpful to go through your research, or to read related items, to see if any phrase, picture, or image suddenly sparks your interest. Sometimes when writers get stuck at the research stage, they're instinctively looking for the dramatic center, that key that can unlock their inspiration.

Yet for all its power and importance, your dramatic center is only one criterion for how you should select ideas to write about. In the next chapter, we'll discuss the other crucial element you must consider before you commit to a story idea.

The Most Valuable Tool You Have

QUESTIONS

In trying to determine what the dramatic center of your story is, here are some questions you can ask yourself:

1. What is the emotional essence of your story?
2. What draws you to this subject?
3. What truly fascinates you about the material?
     Is it the characters' behavior?
     Their attitudes?
     The problem?
     The situation?
     Their skills?
     How the person solves the problem?
     Why that person is facing the problem?
4. Why is this material important to you?
5. Do you feel that the world needs to hear what you have to say? Why?
6. What new insight do you have into the topic?
7. What have you got to say that hasn't been said before?
8. Do you really believe what your story's saying?
9. Why are you writing this story?
10. What do you want your audience to feel?
11. What new understanding do you want your audience to gain?
12. Why are you the right person to write this idea?
13. What about the story idea excites you?
14. Why did you decide to write this story?
15. What about the concept do you think is its biggest hook?
16. How do you want your audience to feel about this story?
17. How do you want your audience to feel during this story?
18. Do you really want to write this idea or is it one you think you should write?
19. How do you feel about spending six months or a year with this topic?

FIVE

Is This the Roller Coaster You Want to Build?

L et's say you have an idea that really appeals to you. The next step is deciding if that is a roller coaster you really want to build. Do you really believe that the core idea behind your roller coaster is commercial enough to help you achieve your career goals? It's a crucial decision, because the basic idea of your screenplay is probably the single most important element in determining how it will fare in the marketplace. It's central to make sure you are being realistic in your assessments, and that you can live with the results.

Some writers don't care what happens to their stories once they get them down on paper, but many do. They have very specific ideas about being a major Hollywood screenwriter, or a small independent filmmaker; either way is fine as long as you are honest with yourself about how well it fits your career goals.

Is This the Roller Coaster You Want to Build?

The search for these answers will usually either confirm your instincts that the idea you've chosen is a good one for you to write or strengthen your suspicion that it might not be an idea for you to pursue. The quicker you can get a realistic gauge about how much you believe in an idea, the better, because how much you believe in the idea, how confident you are that you can bring it to life, and how proud you expect to feel about the final outcome will all have an impact on every aspect of your writing. In fact, your level of commitment to the idea is often the key factor in determining whether you ever complete your screenplay. Even after your script is written, your commitment will continue to influence its chances of success because selling a script is hard work, and most writers eventually give up unless they are genuinely excited about and proud of their screenplay.

The core questions you must ask—and be determined to answer—are "Is this an idea to which I can really commit?" "Will this idea appeal to the kind of audience I want to attract?" "Will this script position me as the kind of writer I want to become?" Honestly exploring these issues can be a little unsettling for many writers, and often they are eager to hurry past this stage of the creative process. I suggest, however, that you do whatever emotional homework it takes to be really certain that you are comfortable with your choice of material and its likelihood of commercial success, or the resulting ambiguity will cause bleed-through that will haunt you every step of the way!

The function of your story concept is like that of the barker at a carnival: its purpose is to attract potential riders to your roller coaster. Ideas deemed "commercial" are the ones in which some buyer in the marketplace feels confident that audiences will be eager to ride; "uncommercial" means that the same party has decided a ticket to that roller coaster would be too hard to sell.

With that kind of life-and-death outcome hanging in the balance, many writers are convinced that the only way to succeed is to write something commercial, whether or not that kind of story genuinely appeals to them. They disregard ideas for which they feel genuine passion and commit themselves instead to mainstream genre pieces; ironically, it is that very sacrifice that often prevents them from having the success they crave.

Yet most writers have only the vaguest sense of what the commercial realities are, and they make crucial decisions on inaccurate or incomplete information. In this chapter, we're going to examine some of the Hollywood myths and generalities, and see which hold up under more detailed scrutiny.

What Hollywood wants is films that make money. The object, of course, is to make millions, but at the very least studios and producers want a reasonable return on their investment. That means attracting an initial audience that finds the experience satisfying enough to recommend it to friends, thus allowing the film to stay in theaters long enough to become profitable. Statistics suggest that the big box office hits tend to have an audience profile of viewers mainly in their teens and early twenties, and repeat ticket sales are usually necessary to create a huge profit.

That all sounds simple enough, but what does that actually tell you? Is it possible to take that kind of "statistical" information and translate it into a recipe that guarantees success? Are there really common denominators that are always true for attracting and satisfying viewers? If so, what are they? What exactly does the industry mean by the term *commercial*?

It's a question I hear all the time. In fact, more than once during the last few years a frustrated writer has stormed up to me and wailed, "Just tell me what's commercial, so I can write the stupid thing!"

▪ Commercial = List of Ingredients? ▪

One reason this topic can be so frustrating for writers is that they are often looking for a list of plot elements that are carved in stone and never vary— steamy sex scenes, great action sequences, exciting car chases, happy endings, or superstar casting. While it's true that many successful films have those kinds of big moments, it's also easy to think of films like *Hudson Hawk* that had these elements and still failed. Meanwhile, what about hits like *Driving Miss Daisy*? It can really strain your imagination to find a list of common plot points among *Home Alone*, *The Godfather*, *Batman*, and *Terms of Endearment*.

In fact, it's clear from studying box office winners that actual plot ingredients vary tremendously, and the more you study the box office and TV ratings reports, the more you will see that this is true. That's because individual ingredients—no matter how good they look on paper—can only provide momentary interest; they have never been, nor will be, enough to guarantee commercial success. To be a genuine hit, it's not enough that a TV show get a good sampling of curious viewers when it first comes on the air, or for a film to attract viewers during its first weekend in release. To stay in the marketplace long enough to make money, a cinematic story must satisfy viewers so that they will come back again or recommend it to their friends. In order to do that, it must provide a compelling story experience. So what makes a film emotionally successful is not just what happens in the *positive space* on the screen, but what happens in the audience's *negative space* as well.

▪ Commercial = Potential Blockbuster? ▪

Another way the marketplace uses the word "commercial" is to describe the big-budget extravaganzas like *Batman*, *Jurassic Park*, *Lethal Weapon*, and *The Addams Family*, which are usually a major studio's attempt to hit a box office home run. These are often geared toward young viewers (who often return again and again), and the reason they are so crucial to the industry is that these blockbusters often keep studios going financially, since as a general rule only one film in five makes big money at the box office.

Yet contrary to popular opinion, a film doesn't have to be a potential blockbuster to get made. In fact, would-be blockbusters make up only a small portion of the approximately four to five hundred Hollywood films released each year. The entire film-distribution business is built on the acknowledgment that every film is not a blockbuster. That's why, in addition to the mass-market strategies used to launch films like *Batman*, *Dick Tracy*, and *Jurassic Park*, there are also entire branches of the distribution business devoted to marketing limited release films like *Fried Green Tomatoes* (which can develop mass-market appeal if they get enough time to generate strong word-of-mouth support), specialty films like *The Player* (which are only targeted to specific regions or markets), or art films (foreign films and the like).

One reason not to drive yourself crazy writing *Lethal Weapon 10* if you would prefer to write a quiet story about farmers is that numerically your chances of success are actually better in the non-blockbuster portions of the market. Another reason not to force yourself to write that kind of film is that when you are competing for one of those blockbuster slots, you'll be up against the toughest competition in the industry. Studios have so much money riding on these films that they look for anything that can increase the movie's chances of success, which often means dealing with writers whose track records are already established.

Meanwhile, the producers of smaller films have just as many marketplace concerns to worry about, not the least of which is budget. You can actually weaken your chances of getting your farmer script produced if you include a lot of extraneous car chases, crowd scenes, special effects, or other glitzy elements in an effort to be commercial, since such additions can easily make the film too expensive to produce.

▪ Commercial = High Concept? ▪

Another connotation of commercial is the industry term *high concept*, which means that the skeletal idea is enough to indicate to viewers what kind of emotional experience the movie will provide without needing to know small details. For example, in *The Terminator*, the basic idea that an indestructible monster from the future has come back to kill someone tells viewers all they need to know about the thrills and excitement such a movie is likely to provide. "Soft" concepts, on the other hand, are movies dependent on the personality of the people involved. In *Fried Green Tomatoes*, for example, there is no way for viewers to anticipate what kind of emotional experience the movie will produce unless they know something about the characters and the details of their lives.

The main reason that high concept ideas can be such an advantage in the marketplace is that they are easy to convey. Promotion budgets are very expensive. The faster advertisers can communicate an idea to potential viewers, the less money producers will have to shell out before they can begin to make a profit. However, the concept of a cinematic story usually has the most impact when audiences first hear about it; after that, word of mouth tends to be more responsible for getting other viewers to watch the story.

▪ Commercial = Box Office Trends? ▪

Another approach that's often used to define what's commercial is to watch what's currently doing well at the box office or in the TV ratings. As a result, sexy thrillers are suddenly commercial after the success of *Basic Instinct*, or sci-fi series are the newest trend after the successful launch of "Deep Space Nine," so it seems like a safe bet to start cranking out some new version of whatever's hot. However, that's probably one of the worst mistakes you can make, because by the time you finish your screenplay, the industry will be so flooded with similar stories that your idea will not only seem dated but perhaps even cliché.

The entertainment marketplace, just like the financial marketplace, is driven by supply and demand. An idea that's excitingly original when it first appears quickly loses its appeal once it becomes familiar. The same "here today, gone tomorrow" quality is true of almost any other trendy element of a screenplay, and if you think about it for a moment, you'll understand why. In Chapter Two we talked about how audiences are hungry for new sensations. The neophile passion is insatiable; viewers are always on a quest for new information. The trouble is that the thrill of a particular novelty can last only so long before viewers get bored and start hungering for something else.

Statistics show that more than half of the biggest box office hits are genres that were *not* currently popular when the movie arrived on the scene, and the same novelty factor is true of hit television series as well. In fact, if you're going to use the current box office/TV ratings as any kind of gauge in deciding what to write, you should look for the genres that *aren't* currently being done, because the marketplace pendulum always swings. Viewers are always developing a hunger for what they're not getting.

▪ Commercial = Hot Topics? ▪

The same hunger for the new that affects a genre's appeal also affects the audience's interest in provocative topics. How society feels at any given time about a controversial social issue, for instance, can have profound impact on your script's commercial potential. Obviously you can't always predict exactly how attitudes will change in the future, but there are somewhat recognizable cycles that you can train yourself to notice. Most issues move through our society like waves, and a script's commercial potential will be powerfully affected by when in this cycle it appears.

The fastest cycle is that of a *social fad*, which is why cinematic roller coasters that are based on fads are a bad bet. Features like *Lambada* can take so long to develop that the fad's popularity is gone before the movie is even released.

The cycle of *social issues* tends to last longer. Early in the cycle, when the level of public knowledge or comfort level is low, a script dealing with that topic will often get rejected for being too controversial. The same script can suddenly seem highly commercial if it hits the marketplace just as the subject is coming to national consciousness (often because the subject is a "deep, dark secret" that has never been discussed openly before). However, societal attitudes adjust quickly, and once the wave crests, the audience grows bored with that topic unless your script offers a new viewpoint or twist. Eventually such topics are so familiar to viewers that they become part of the background of a story; then the same cycle, on a different topic, starts all over again.

Therefore, the most important consideration when choosing possible topics is not whether they are "hot," but whether there is something about the topic that would actively attract viewers. It could be curiosity, novelty, or fantasy fulfillment, or a life affirming "feel good" experience, but the important thing is to make sure that the subject has an obvious component that would make viewers want to spend time in that world.

• Commercial = The "More!" Mentality? •

It's difficult to predict what's going to be the next big social trend, so the industry has developed other ways to ensure exciting sensations for viewers by finding technologies and provocative visual elements that give the audience an opportunity for *more!* "Moreness" can occur in the area of action, special effects, sound technologies, visual techniques, sexuality, or any other sensual element of the story. Yet even *more!* has only temporary appeal because its uniqueness is only a matter of degrees. For example, *Terminator 2* was on the cutting edge of technology, and it took millions of dollars and countless man-hours to achieve. The movie was dazzling and unique at the time, but now viewers have seen it; already they want *more!* The same is true of nudity, violence, shock value, or any other factor that was once considered to be on the cutting edge.

The basis of the entire *more! mentality* is the desire to create a sense of "event" that gets viewers "out of their heads" and completely absorbed in the world of the story. But does it usually work? How many films or television shows have you really enjoyed to such an extent? How many times have you felt that ideal sensation of being totally involved?

Probably not very often. That's because hot spots of sensation are not emotionally satisfying unless they are strung together in such a way that they develop a meaningful "big picture" for viewers. So rather than worrying about whether your idea is commercial, you should be focusing on whether your idea can really provoke strong, exciting, satisfying emotions for viewers. Ultimately what really matters is the quality of the roller-coaster ride.

So don't look at the external ingredients of successful films and TV shows; look at the roller-coaster experience it provides instead. Audiences go to films to experience sensations, visceral thrills, and emotional revelations, so any story that will provoke strong emotions in viewers has a better chance of being produced.

For example, look at some of the top grossing films of all time:

STAR WARS	THE EXORCIST
E.T.	THE RETURN OF THE JEDI
JAWS	THE EMPIRE STRIKES BACK
THE SOUND OF MUSIC	THE STING
THE GODFATHER	JURASSIC PARK
GONE WITH THE WIND	BATMAN

See? The one thing these hits have in common is the ability to provoke strong emotion in viewers.

So the bad news is that there are no absolutes when it comes to the tangible ingredients of what's commercial. But the good news is that once you accept that essential truth you can stop worrying about trying to be commercial, and learn to develop other criteria for deciding whether or not you want to pursue a screenplay idea.

I can just hear you gasping now, but before you panic, think about what I'm saying. I am not recommending that you ignore the realities of the marketplace. Playing ostrich about the financial considerations in an industry that lives and dies by box office numbers and TV ratings is a sure-fire prescription for frustration and disappointment, but so is searching for a magical formula or list of ingredients that simply doesn't exist. What's important is that you make informed decisions in a realistic evaluation of your idea's commercial potential, and then decide if you can make peace with yourself about that outcome or not.

The best of all possible worlds, of course, is to find an idea that you would love to write about and that you are also confident has strong commercial appeal. However, many writers simply are not drawn to such mainstream stories, and if that's true of you, here are some thoughts about various available alternatives.

First of all, make sure you do your homework. Research the marketplace and find out which companies make and distribute the kind of film you want to write. There may be more of a market for your story than you originally assumed. If there is, study those films and see if you can identify the kinds of budgets, financing, and other production considerations that they have in common. If you can't find a market segment into which your script fits neatly, decide if you still want to pursue writing that idea.

The worst of all possible alternatives is to fool yourself about your script's chances of success at the beginning of the process and then become bitter at the end if it gets rejected for reasons that could have been easily predicted if you'd really been honest with yourself. Another mistake I see writers make is to choose an idea they know has only limited commercial appeal, then either force it into some commercial mold or eliminate its most distinctive aspects. The result of such decisions are scripts that are neither fish nor fowl; they are neither well suited to the external marketplace demands, nor do they provide the writer with the internal satisfaction of having been true to that inner voice.

If you think you have a great idea but are genuinely concerned that the idea isn't marketable, then don't write it now. Wait until you have more success and there is some demand for your work. Another viable alternative if your story contains a real standout character is to try to get your script into the hands of a major box office star who may have some interest in playing that kind of role. Studios will sometimes attempt riskier projects when major stars are attached.

Also try to dig deep and be honest about your real motives for writing the particular script. Do you only want to use it as a showcase for your writing ability, or are you determined only to invest your time and effort in a script you feel confident will sell? If it's the latter case, here are some ways to work on developing an "educated gut" about the factors that can heighten a script's commercial appeal.

1. A Matter of Degree

First of all, try thinking of commercial considerations not as black or white absolutes, but as a matter of degree. The more your story appeals to the four basic hungers we discussed in Chapter Two (new information, emotional bonding, conflict resolution, and the promise of completion), the better your chances are of someone in the industry sensing that your screenplay would be the blueprint for a great roller coaster.

Another consideration is how well your story takes advantage of the medium. Is the jeopardy visual, or is all the emotional power in the dialogue? Are there great moments of excitement, or is the story more intellectually provocative without stirring strong emotion? Is it the kind of roller coaster whose thrills are "repeatable" (for example, such complex adventures as *Star Wars* or *Jaws*), or is it a roller coaster that builds to one startling discovery (such as *Body Heat*) and then loses a lot of its impact once the audience knows the surprise?

2. Don't Copy the Past

Many books and classes about screenwriting use existing scripts or films as templates, but there are several reasons why that's not necessarily a good idea.

First of all, copying existing roller coasters (always placing key turning points in the same place, for example) means that you will ultimately just end up building the same roller coaster again and again. Since audiences crave new experiences, that's exactly what they don't want.

Additionally, just because a film or television show has been produced doesn't mean it's a good example of success. If you do your homework and explore the behind-the-scenes story about many a hit, you may soon discover that it was the financial deal, or star casting, or existing production commitments, or other non–script-related issues that were really the determining factor in getting a particular script produced *even though the participants knew that the screenplay itself was flawed.* Conversely, sometimes the original script was terrific, but, like that old saying about how a horse designed by committee ends up looking like a camel, what you see on the screen is the result of choices and compromises that make it quite different from the script that originally got the producers excited. Therefore, if you blindly copy an existing roller coaster without doing your homework, you just may end up copying someone else's mistakes.

3. Study Sleepers

Studying sleepers is a good way to develop your awareness of what makes a story roller coaster successful with viewers. *Sleepers* is the industry term for films that don't get a lot of promotion but manage to find their audience anyway. The reason it's better to study films that have not been the subject of one of Hollywood's major publicity campaigns is that when you try to track the emotional effectiveness of films like the first *Batman*, it's hard to separate the appeal of the actual roller-coaster experience from the carefully orchestrated "buzz." Sleepers, however, have no such launching pad to put them in orbit. It's only the fact that viewers find them so satisfying that allows them to survive and even flourish. *Fried Green Tomatoes*, *Chariots of Fire*, *Home Alone*, and *The Crying Game* are movies that enjoyed this kind of success; "Seinfeld," "Cheers," and "Hill Street Blues" were television sleepers.

4. Study Movie Previews

Next time you go to a movie, pay close attention to the coming attractions, as well as your reaction to them. Such trailers give you a chance to study the essence of a movie's concept. Notice which ones catch your interest and which ones leave you cold. Train yourself to articulate your reasoning, so that it will rise up to your consciousness and not remain simply instinctive. Then make note of your reactions and compare them to what happens at the box office when the film is released. Were you right about its audience appeal? Were you wrong? Can you figure out why? If not, make a point of seeing the film yourself, and see if the quality of the roller coaster had anything to do with its unexpected performance at the box office.

5. Study Failure

Studying box office failures is also very important. When you hear about a film that has failed at the box office despite the fact that it seemed to have everything going for it commercially, make a point of seeing it before it disappears. That way you can study its roller-coaster construction carefully to find why it disappointed riders, you can analyze whether the promotional campaign made promises the film could never have delivered, or whether the concept itself was innately flawed.

6. Anticipate the Future

We've talked before about the social cycles that influence a topic's commercial appeal. If you are interested in writing stories dealing with such social issues, it's important to train yourself to look forward.

Look in obscure places for the issues that are on the upswing before they become too well known. Once such topics are on the talk-show circuit, for example, they are already becoming too familiar to be exciting much longer, and that is especially true if you are thinking of writing for features, which tend to take several years to go from the first draft to the screen.

Make a point of reading little-known magazines, medical journals, law journals, local newspapers, technical and scientific journals, science fiction magazines, and computer billboards for small news items. What you're looking for are stories that provide a new slant on an area of established interest, which is just about as close to a magic formula for a commercial idea as you can get.

Is This the Roller Coaster You Want to Build?

QUESTIONS

Once you think you've found an idea which you could really be interested in, here is a list of questions to consider:

1. Does your idea create an exciting roller coaster?
   Are its thrills repeatable?
2. Does it provoke strong emotions?
   Are there big emotional stakes?
   Does it have great moments?
3. Does it tap into universal emotions?
4. How does it fulfill the neophile/neophobe hunger?
   Does it tell viewers something new?
   Does it touch on an area of established curiosity?
   Does it provide a new slant?
5. Does it go to the next step?
6. Is there a reason for viewers to want to spend time in that world?
   Is it life-affirming?
   Is there an underlying idea that the viewers will want to believe?
7. Does it provide fantasy fulfillment?
8. Is it a star vehicle?
   Is there a character for viewers to bond with?
9. Is it "high concept"?
   Will it be easy to promote?
10. Will it appeal to young viewers?
    Why?
11. Is it in keeping with today's sensibilities?
    Is it a topic affected by current social cycles?
12. Does it fit into an identifiable portion of the market?
13. What is your goal for this script? To use it as a writing sample, or to get it made?

SIX

Structure: Designing Your Roller Coaster

L et's say that you now have an idea for a roller coaster that you really can commit to. What is the next step?

Imagine that a major theme park hired you to create a new roller-coaster ride. The first thing you would consider is how to arrive at a general sense of the kind of overall experience you want to create for the riders. The next thing would be to study the land, get your impressions of the general layout, and imagine which styles of roller coaster might work. Eventually you would develop a specific idea of the kind of roller coaster you want to create; only then would you begin to figure out exactly how to combine the various components to construct the actual ride.

Structure: Designing Your Roller Coaster

The same dynamic is true for the structure of screenplays. Once you've selected an idea, it is tremendously helpful to develop a sense of what overall pattern you want to create *before* you start selecting the other components of your script. Yet many writers never think about the cumulative "big picture" as an individual creative choice, or they assume that all they have to do to create a compelling ride is develop their basic idea into a logical, cohesive plot. However, both of those approaches allow the audience's highs and lows to occur almost at random, and the resulting structure is often so erratic that it prevents the audience from achieving the emotional build and release that you desire and they crave.

A phrase you often hear in Hollywood is "A screenplay is structure," which means that the real power, cohesiveness, and impact of a screenplay can be assessed by how well its big picture pattern works. Your goal as a writer is to create a specific series of emotions in your audience, and every aspect of your screenplay, including the logical organization of events, is just a means toward that end, so the sooner you begin to have a sense of its shape and texture, the sooner you can begin to focus your creative energies on selecting the right components.

The reason for structure's dominance is that the big picture emotional ride determines whether the audience will achieve a sense of catharsis, which in turn determines whether they will find the story emotionally satisfying or not. Humans need catharsis. They need the release, the venting of emotions, the sweeping yet pleasurable sense of being completely spent after their emotional level has built to a peak, then subsided. Deep in the human genetic memory people recognize the truth of the pattern of life and death in which sensations move to a peak and then fade away. Experiences such as sex, joy, grief, and pain are all patterns of tension and release as primal and fundamental as existence itself, so they crave them. But humans don't often have an opportunity to experience catharsis so completely in life; consequently, they crave it in stories.

Humans are so sensitive to cathartic patterns that they hunger for them at the deepest level, beyond words, logic, or rational analysis. One of the best examples of how primal the hunger for emotional release can be is music. Music has no words, no ideas, no plot, and no facts, yet if you listen to a beautiful piece of music, you will often experience a perception of perfect structure.

One of my favorite pieces is *Opus Eleven: Adagio for Strings* by Samuel Barber, the music that director Oliver Stone chose to play under the final scene of *Platoon*. It is a deeply moving piece, about seven minutes long, which starts with a deep, low poignant sound, moves up in waves to a heartbreaking crescendo, then fades away. It is a virtually perfect example of structure.

But if there are no words, no ideas, no characters, no events—in fact none of the things that are necessary to create a story—what creates the structure in music? It is the interrelationship of elements that creates a tension due to building emotional states that demand climax, completion, and release. Those emotional sensations are created in the people listening to music as their logical and emotional energies are directed at comparing and grouping the individual elements into categories, hearing simultaneous or sequential groupings, comparing proximity, similarity, continuity, and direction, all of which suggests that structure is the end result of a complex network of interactions.

Yet many writers have been taught that structure is created simply by the format of the screenplay (such as a television movie having seven acts, or a one-hour drama having four), a likable central character, the right chronology of events, and turning points that occur in specific places. Defining dramatic structure as a list of ingredients however, is like saying that because a house has windows, doors, shelves, and floors, a house *is* windows and doors and shelves and floors. While it's certainly true that a well-built house will contain those parts, they only combine to create a house if they are used in a very specific relationship to each other.

That's how it is with dramatic structure. Ultimately, structure is not a separate element but rather the overall shape of the audience's building emotional response to all the ingredients of your story. If the audience is increasingly intrigued by the plot, emotionally involved with the characters, eager to know what's going to happen next because of well-focused momentum, and saturated with exciting use of style, they then experience a compelling and unified ride that takes them through an exciting build to climax and resolve. Only when both the audience's emotional and logical energies have been harnessed and focused can they experience real catharsis.

In the end, structure is both the result of what occurs to an audience's emotions if all the other elements of a screenplay are performing their functions well and the starting point from which you begin as you work out the specific contents of your roller coaster. How you develop the other elements of your roller coaster will be determined by your structural choice.

▪ Finding the Right Structure ▪

Sometimes you can find clarity about your structure almost as soon as you determine the story idea; sometimes your understanding evolves slowly as you hunt for your dramatic center, research your topic, or immerse yourself in a variety of possibilities before the best option makes itself clear to you.

However, by the time you are writing your final drafts of a screenplay, you need to be fully conscious of the pattern of emotional highs and lows you are trying to create for your viewers, so that you can use both your creativity and your craft to ensure that it is working. The sooner you begin to develop some sense of what that overall pattern is in your story, the more successfully you can create a unified whole.

One item you can think about is the pattern of change that most interests you; another way to focus your creative energies is to ask yourself if you can envision even the vaguest outline of *key moments of change*. Those are the moments when the direction, speed, or texture of a roller coaster suddenly take an exciting turn, and these are often the first hint you get of how you see your story's structure.

For example, one pattern that can be theatrical is a series of seemingly small changes which might not even be noticed at first but suddenly add up to a huge change; such films as *The Andromeda Strain* and *Invasion of the Body Snatchers* fit this pattern. In contrast, sometimes the pattern of change is exciting because of its extremes. *Friday the Thirteenth* and *Blame It on Rio* have almost continuous patterns of ups and downs, while *All the President's Men*

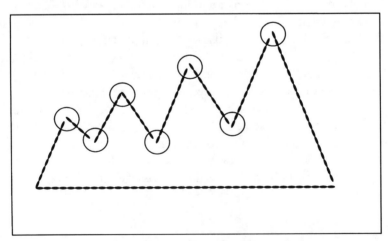

Key Moments of Change

simply builds incrementally upward, as does the classic screwball comedy *Bringing Up Baby*.

Sometimes the key moment of change occurs after a crucial discovery is made, such as in *The Conversation*, which contrasts many seemingly small incidents in the beginning of the story with a stunning revelation near the end. Other films create a series of building revelations, such as in *Witness*, when Harrison Ford first realizes that the killer is actually a member of the police force, then later learns that his own trusted boss is also corrupt. Some films focus on building a relentless sense of urgency and danger, such as *The Hand That Rocks the Cradle*, while others seem to start out smoothly and then become unexpectedly dangerous in the second half, such as *Body Heat* or *No Way Out*.

Whatever the pattern, the more your structure can convey the texture of those essential realizations, the more effective your story will be for the audience, on both the conscious and subconscious level. For example, in *The Day of the Jackal*, the dramatic center of the idea had to do with the ever-present tension of the professional assassin. He was on a relentless mission, and there was no real emotional release for him until the mission was done. Understanding that the sensation of building tension was crucial to the story, the plot contained several murders, but the script's roller coaster was constructed to minimize the theatrical impact of each scene in order to maintain the taut, tense upward build of emotional tension in the audience. Thus what could have been a roller coaster that looked like this:

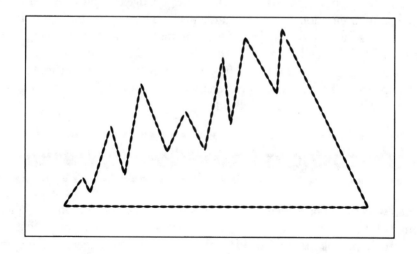

ended up looking like this:

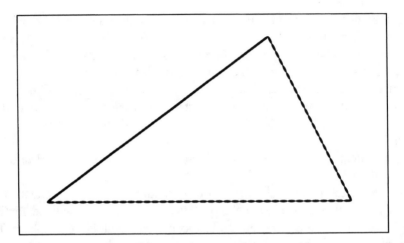

thus forcing the audience to endure the same emotional tension and hunger for the eventual resolution.

Having a sense of your structure first is so useful because it gives you a concrete image for which to aim. Thus having at least an initial understanding of the dynamic of change in your story is crucial, because it affects all the other components of your screenplay. As you develop your story more and more, you will see that the key changes that affect the sequence of events become the core logic of your plot, while tracking the changes within the characters become their emotional arcs. The audience's change in its understanding of the story is the foundation for creating momentum, and intensifying those sensations of change becomes the basis for using style effectively.

So as you begin to think about the specific plot events or characters in your screenplay, having a sense of what changes they will undergo will help you incorporate them into the overall ride.

Choosing a Roller-Coaster Design

Often writers will have a visceral sense of what some of those shifts might be long before they have chosen the exact plot and character points that will eventually provoke them. For example, here's how the same story material might result in strikingly different roller coasters.

Structure: Designing Your Roller Coaster

Let's say that five different writers were hired to write screenplays about the same failed marriage. One writer, who was fascinated by the slow, steady, incremental build of destructiveness and anger within the couple, would probably build a roller coaster that looks something like this:

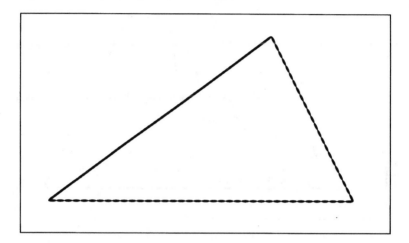

The writer who was intrigued by the contrast between the couple's seemingly idyllic beginning, which suddenly and mysteriously turned vengeful one night, would probably like the audience to experience a ride more like this:

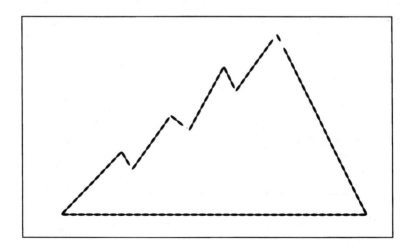

Structure: Designing Your Roller Coaster

The script created by the writer who was convinced that the marriage was never really happy might plant startling hints which become a larger and larger portion of the couple's life and create this kind of sensation for viewers:

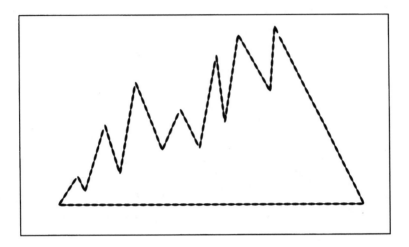

Meanwhile, the script written by the author who decided to begin the screenplay with the couple's violent, final breakup, then flash back to the beginning of the story and work forward from that point would want to create the following kind of roller-coaster experience for viewers:

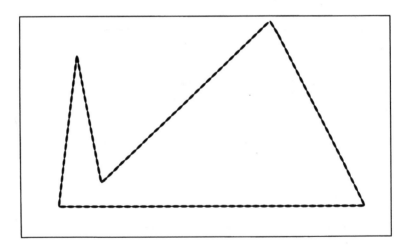

Structure: Designing Your Roller Coaster

The script written by the author who was intrigued by the image of a marriage falling apart in small moments, never big fights, might build a structure like this:

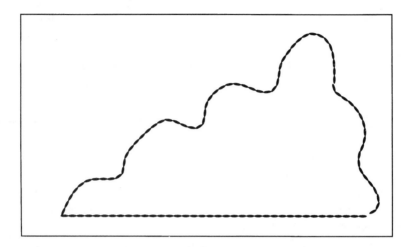

Once you truly understand structure, you can see how profoundly this creative choice affects every other aspect of writing a screenplay, which is why I disagree so strongly with formulas that tell you where you must place certain turning points, or in what order certain events must occur. By predetermining the incidents of your story, they are telling you to build the same basic roller coaster again and again. Yet the same roller coaster again and again is exactly what viewers *don't want*. The audience wants new thrills, new sensations, and new information; riding the same roller coaster again and again ultimately gets boring, no matter how well designed, because it becomes too easy for the audience to anticipate the ride.

Sharing Your Excitement

As you can see, the overall structure of the story is much more dependent on the writer's own sense of excitement about the topic than the actual topic. Consequently, you must decide exactly what excites you about the topic and what sequence of emotions would best convey that excitement to the viewers.

Structure: Designing Your Roller Coaster

You will find that there is a direct connection between *your* dramatic center of your story, which is the specific angle of the idea which excites you, and the overall structure of the piece that you want to build for your audience. That's because it's exactly that thrill, that jolt, or that sweeping sense of ecstasy which makes the material appealing to you and therefore lets you know what sensations you want to create for your audience. Without that kind of visceral target to reach for, screenwriting can become an exercise in logic that is too far removed from its emotional roots to be really compelling.

Yet despite its importance, your dramatic center is actually only one sensation, one revelation, one emotion. Getting viewers into that emotional state involves creating a series of emotional transitions that lead them to that crucial moment.

Humans don't experience emotions in isolation, but in context or juxtaposition with other emotional states. Therefore, knowing what emotional state you ultimately want your audience to have can help you develop a sense of what other emotional states you will need to provoke in them in order for them to experience your dramatic center.

For example, betrayal is a painful emotional state, and can therefore be quite dramatic. However, the actual moment of betrayal is only the end result of a series of previous emotional states, such as the pleasure of getting to know someone new, developing a friendship with that person, thinking that the person is trustworthy, taking a big chance with that person, and then finding yourself betrayed.

Some of the most intense moments in life are those moments of change when people shift in their attitudes or assessments from one state of mind to another. The more certain people are of their assessment of the situation, the more powerful the shift can be; in fact, the moment of betrayal is even more powerful when the previous moments of trust and sharing are deep and intense.

The same is true with stories. It is actually the shift in emotional states, the progression of feelings, that make a story dynamic, and so, as soon as possible you need to understand exactly what series of emotional transitions are necessary to convey the core dynamics of your story.

It's important to remember that you want your viewers to *experience* your world view, rather than just observe it passively or think about it later. Making sure that you are creating the kind of "felt experience" that best conveys your dramatic center demands that you stay focused on the audience's emotional reactions rather than solely on your story's logical order.

QUESTIONS

Here are some function questions to help focus your creative energies:

1. Do you have a clear sense of the overall shape of the roller coaster you are trying to design?
2. What is the dramatic center of your story?
3. What pattern of change intrigues you?
4. Do you have a clear sense of the overall shape of roller coaster that would best convey those sensations?
5. What do you want your audience to feel?
6. What textures would best convey that emotional quality? Smooth? Jagged? Abrupt? Slow? Fast?
7. What previous emotional states would be necessary in order to make those key moments more effective?
8. Can you think of any similar story roller coasters?
9. Did you like the sensation that roller coaster created? Why?
10. What is the difference between that roller coaster and the one you want to build?

SEVEN

Plot: Building Your Roller Coaster

L et's say you now have an idea what shape you want your roller coaster to be. What would happen if you simply hung the track up in the air? Obviously it wouldn't last a minute. In order for the track to function effectively, the intended design must be translated into an actual construction.

The same is true for a story roller coaster. The structure is your intended design, but the plot is what actually creates the audience highs and lows by presenting story information that provokes emotion. Therefore, you want to select and arrange the story information in a way that creates, arouses, and intensifies the audience's emotional involvement until it builds to climax and release.

Writers think that a plot is just "what happens," so by the time they've chosen an idea, they already have a sense of what the events should be. But just because an image or scene occurs to you while pondering your story doesn't mean that it must be included in the screenplay. Thus it is essential that you develop clear criteria about what to include and what to eliminate as you begin to translate your concept into a plot.

Plot: Building Your Roller Coaster

The first thing is to understand the difference between plot and story. Story is all of the potential information about your idea, while plot is your selection and arrangement of pertinent information chosen to dramatize your dramatic center. For example, in my Lizzie script, the story could begin at the birth of her parents and continue to Lizzie's death or even beyond. However, such a straightforward chronology of events would not provide the focus and clarity needed to bring a unique vision of the story to life. In order to separate the details of plot, you must identify the central issues, causes, obstacles, and ramifications that will express your take on the story.

How Plot Addresses the Audience's Four Needs

Your plot's primary function is to examine the process of *conflict resolution*, which involves confronting the many challenges and problems created by change. Since it is often difficult for people to attain clarity about the changes and conflicts in their own lives, exploring similar issues in a fictional setting can allow them to see from different perspectives, thus providing insight and understanding.

However, you also need to make sure your plot addresses the other core emotional needs of the audience. It should include enough *new information* to hold their interest, allowing them to glimpse other realities. This is what supplies much of the appeal of films like *Cliffhanger, Marooned, Pretty Woman*, and other stories that move viewers into worlds and sensations they may never experience on their own. Plot also must help viewers *bond* to the story. Presenting a central conflict pertinent to the viewers' lives will let an audience feel a personal connection to the story.

The last of the four core needs your plot must fulfill is *completion*, so that the audience can experience the satisfaction of building to a climax, then resolving. One of the fundamental demands audiences make on stories is that stories should "make life make sense"; therefore the ending of the story is critical to the audience's overall level of enjoyment of it. Because of the audience's hunger for closure, a plot that leaves unanswered questions won't be satisfying.

▪ Moving from Inspiration to Plot ▪

Many writers lose the clarity of their original vision as they struggle to create a cohesive and coherent plotline. The "big picture" fades as they try to solve a million smaller details, and the result is often a choppy, erratic screenplay that no longer addresses the aspects of the idea that first drew the writer to it. To avoid this problem, you must make conscious and consistent choices about how to use your screen time to tell the actual story you were inspired to tell. Therefore, it is crucial that you fully understand what your screenplay is really about.

Conventional wisdom says that stories are about conflict, but as we discussed in the last chapter, the reason the aspects of change reflected in your story's structure are so crucial is that stories are really about the deeper, primal emotional dilemma centering on humans' fear of, yet need to, change. Conflict can create momentary excitement because of its theatricality, but its genuine power comes from the fact that it intensifies the likelihood of change.

Change is potent because it is the essential dynamic of life itself. It is the one common denominator that all humans face: bodies change, seasons change, lives change, relationships change, feelings change, locations change, and technologies change, so people must learn to cope with change if they want to survive. Yet as universal as change may be, people often resist it because they fear the unknown. Thus the tension between the need for change and the fear of it can be fascinating territory for stories.

In order to decide what aspect of change you want to dramatize in your screenplay, you must determine which kind of change most intrigues you and why you think that encounter with change should be told. Your plot can center on four kinds of change, all of which may appeal to viewers because they recognize such dilemmas in their own lives. *Internal change* deals with conflicts and issues inside the central character, as in *Amadeus* or *Hamlet*. Another kind of change is *interpersonal change*, in films like *Kramer vs. Kramer* or *High Noon*, in which change is caused by other characters. *Societal change*, such as in *The China Syndrome*, deals with people facing issues on a larger scale, while *situational change*, as in *Jurassic Park* or *The Towering Inferno*, deals with people's need to confront external challenges.

The *inability to change* can also be dramatized. Examples are the heartbreaking scene at the end of *Ordinary People* when Mary Tyler Moore's character chooses to leave rather than change her ways, or *Othello's* inability to change his assessment of people, which leads to tragedy and death.

Change can be deep within a person, as in *It's a Wonderful Life*, or only in the outward circumstances, as in *National Lampoon's Christmas Vacation*. It can be a positive change, as in *Rocky*, or a tragic change, as in *Sophie's Choice*. Change can occur easily, as in *All of Me*, or after great resistance, as in *Unforgiven*. Sometimes the struggle is to prevent change, as in *The Invasion of the Body Snatchers*, sometimes to cause change, as in *Hunt for Red October*, sometimes to ignore change, as in *Dead Ringers*, and sometimes to adapt to change, as in *Whose Life Is It, Anyway?* It is always the existing or impending change, however, that forces the plot to advance.

The reason you must see exactly what kind of change you want to explore is that your plot encompasses the information necessary to track the central change from beginning to end. Among the decisions you must make are: What kind of change is faced? What is your view of that change? Why is it important? What are its causes? Why did it start? What makes it difficult? How is that change confronted? And what is the outcome?

In order to answer these questions, you must examine your interest in a story idea very carefully. Your dramatic center is the best tool you have for making sure that the plotline you develop will actually yield a screenplay that captures your excitement about the idea, but often the aspect of change that is connected with your dramatic center is hidden beneath the surface.

For example, in my Lizzie script, the conflict might have seemed interpersonal, but it was really about societal repression. The film *Chapter Two* might seem to be about interpersonal conflict, yet it is really about the internal change James Caan's character needs to make in order to commit to his new marriage.

Since the transition from raw creative impulse to concrete plot can be so challenging, let's examine one way to proceed that can ensure you stay on course.

Like a surveyor, you want to be exact about identifying your dramatic center; if you are not, what could seem like a minor inaccuracy at the center of your story at first will put you far off course later on.

▪ The Pivotal Moment of Change ▪

A good way to begin developing your plot is to determine exactly what the pivotal moment of change in your story is. The pivotal moment of change is the moment when the issues affecting the central change are resolved, leading to the external action which is the climax of the story.

Plot: Building Your Roller Coaster

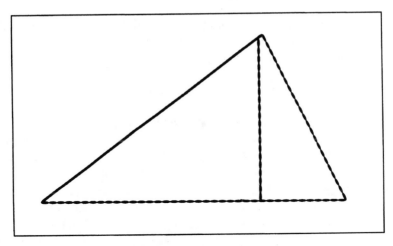

Pivotal Moments of Change

There is always a direct connection between your dramatic center and the pivotal moment of change. For example, if the dramatic center for my Lizzie Borden script is a fascination with her gradual move from sanity to insanity, the pivotal moment would occur when her sanity actually snaps. If my dramatic center is about her relation with her abusive father, the pivotal moment would be when she moves from being able to tolerate the abuse to being unable to control her rage any longer.

Your pivotal moment of change is the key moment you are building to, so once you know exactly where that is, you begin to have clarity about how to use your screen time. For example, if I were writing about Lizzie losing her mind, the information I would select from her story would be those details in which her sanity is more and more in doubt. If I were writing about her obtaining personal freedom from her abusive father, I would select the scenes in which his abuse becomes more and more intolerable. Even though the original source material for the two plotlines is the same, the selection from the entire spectrum of the story of events, characters, and moments would be quite different.

Using your dramatic center almost as the fulcrum of your pivotal moment, you can test the outcome against the visceral sensation signal, the beep-beep-beep of your dramatic center to see how it feels. It's a firm, calm sense of clarity, and once you achieve it, you will feel your creative juices really start to flow.

If you feel genuinely comfortable, then you are ready to go on to the next step. If not, stop now, before proceeding, and double-check your assessments and assumptions thus far. No matter how annoying or unsettling it can be forcing yourself to stay focused on these preliminary decisions, you will not be able to move ahead with confidence and clarity unless you have a firm foundation.

▪ The End Result ▪

Once you feel that you have a grasp of the pivotal moment of change, the next step in developing your plotline is to extend your pivotal moment to see what the end result will be.

For example, in my Lizzie possibilities, the end result based on the pivotal moment in which she lost her sanity would present Lizzie as pitiable, while in the other version, where she revolts against her father's abuse, she would feel triumphant about having ended the oppression that controlled her life. The external action of murder at the end of the story might be the same in both stories, but the emotional texture would be completely different.

Once you have tested your end result, you can ask whether that ending feels right to you. Is that the story you want to write? If so, you can move ahead with confidence. If not, chances are that you don't yet have complete clarity on your dramatic center or pivotal moment of change. So rather than push ahead, focus your energies on clarifying your dramatic center, and then test your findings until you find a pivotal moment and end result that feel absolutely right. Try different variations until you feel total confidence that the plot that would result from these key moments makes the statement you want.

▪ The Starting Point ▪

The next step is to figure out where the plot should begin in order to make the ending feel emotionally and logically satisfying. The polarity between the starting point and the end result sets up the entire arc of your story. Therefore, choosing a beginning that allows the biggest change to occur is a good selection, because the more change that is necessary between the beginning and the end of the story, the more dramatic potential the story has.

In the two versions of the Lizzie story, for instance, the starting point for one would be while she was still quite sane; the other would start when she was abjectly fearful of her father. I may not yet know what the external "packaging" is of the scene, how I am going to dramatize Lizzie's sanity at the beginning of the screenplay, or the pivotal loss of sanity near the end. But once I can envision the emotional longitude and latitude of my story, I do have real clarity about what emotional information I am trying to convey to the audience. Therefore I can begin to select plot events with a clear function in mind.

■ The Dramatic Equation ■

Now you have three key moments in the plotline: the starting point, the pivotal moment of change, and the end result. Feeling genuinely confident about the implied boundaries of your story is crucial, because your plot is a major ingredient in the dramatic equation of your story.

The dramatic equation of a story is its message or statement of values. Boiled down to its essence, your script conveys the message "this person plus this change inevitably equals this outcome." Like an algebraic equation, the internal dynamics of a story must add up and make sense.

In well-crafted short films the dramatic equation is very clear, as it is in short stories. In longer films the central equation is not always so obvious, but the internal logic behind the series of changes must still hold up in order for the audience to feel a sense of clarity and completion. Viewers may not be conscious of the equation; in fact, they usually aren't unless they try to articulate their thoughts about the film. If they do, you may be surprised just how clearly viewers register the central statement of your film.

There's also an important issue of integrity regarding the dramatic equation. You will not feel fully confident unless you believe that the implied statement of your story is essentially true. Even if it's just a comic romp, there is a statement of relative values in every screenplay. Beware that if you don't believe the logic, world view, and values expressed in the outcome message, your internal doubt will cause repeated problems, including creative resistance and even "shutdown."

■ Selecting Your Story Pillars ■

If you are sure that you have defined the boundaries of your story successfully, the next step is selecting and arranging the sequence of events that create, effect, or determine the series of changes that take the screenplay from the starting point to the end result, all of which combine to create your dramatic equation.

For example, if I were dramatizing Lizzie and her father, by now I would have a clear sense of the underlying tension between them; I would then have to decide what would be the best way to present that information to the audience. Should they fight frequently? Live in stoic silence? Does Lizzie reach out for contact while her father turns his back? Keeping the central function in mind as you explore possibilities will allow your mind to create the most exciting and compelling packaging, because it is now clear what the internal criterion is.

Sometimes the external packaging comes to mind first, and you have to search for the deeper issues. Other times, the central change is clear, but exactly what events will best dramatize it is harder to decide. But once you have made your decisions, that information will be conveyed to the audience in *story pillars*—the pieces of information that cause change within the story.

The change may affect the character's status quo (a woman is hit by a car), the character's understanding of the status quo (the woman learns she is dying), the audience's understanding of the status quo (the audience learns that she is dying but she doesn't know), or both. The difference between general plot information and a story pillar is that the story pillars must cause the sensation of change or potential change. Events such as characters brushing their teeth or driving in their cars are not story pillars unless they contain information that might affect the central dynamic of change.

A story pillar's height comes from the intensity of audience reaction; the intensity comes from how much possible change could result from the new information. For example, you might think that a scene in which a building burns is innately more intense than a scene in which a waitress casually declines an offer to have coffee with a customer. However, the burning building could generate no emotional response from viewers if they already know it's on fire, while the scene with the waitress may break your heart if you know that she and the customer are in love and that she will never see him again because he is planning to commit suicide. The power of the second scene comes from the fact that both of their lives will be irrevocably changed by the seemingly small moment.

The sensation I get when a moment of potential change occurs is similar to watching a wall in a Las Vegas casino that displays the numerical odds. Every time a story pillar suggests that there will be a shift, the numbers on the wall flip, sometimes higher, sometimes lower, reflecting the audience's assessment of whether the story's central conflict will be successfully resolved or not. The higher the pillar, the more the numbers change; when the story pillar contains information that results in a small change, maybe only a few numbers flip, but in the really big moments of change, it can seem as though the numbers all over the entire wall are changing!

Load-bearing Pillars

As you begin to get clarity on the key moments of your plot, you may notice that you have the most initial clarity about the *load-bearing pillars* that are the essential story events, the key moments in which the central dynamic definitely shifts.

To understand their importance, try condensing the plot of some film you've seen; the load-bearing pillars are the ones you'll mention because by presenting them you can convey the essence of the story's logic and outcome most concisely. Load-bearing pillars are important because they are the ones that carry the weight of your story. If any were changed or eliminated, the end result would be different, as would the entire dramatic equation.

Often these will be the first key moments of change that become really clear to you as you develop your plotline. You can then decide what other story pillars will be needed to get you from one load-bearing pillar to the next.

For example, in *Fatal Attraction*, Michael Douglas's sexual escapade with Glenn Close was a load-bearing pillar because there wouldn't have been a story without that incident. Yet the story pillar that explained why he was alone that weekend could have included many different explanations, so although it is necessary for the internal logic of the plot, it is not a load-bearing pillar.

Your plot will be made up of the load-bearing pillars. No matter what shape structure you choose for your story roller coaster, it is important that your load-bearing pillars get higher and higher as the screenplay continues. When a writer is successful in creating and increasing the intensity of reaction, the audience can perceive the building tension on both an emotional and intellectual level. For example, think about the first time you saw *Body Heat*, *Fatal Attraction*, or *No Way Out*. The sensation as the pillars become higher and higher is a large part of the excitement and success of these films.

▪ Creating Pillars of Increasing Height ▪

There are seven approaches that can give pillars added height: how much is at stake, how much jeopardy exists, how significant the obstacle is, how desperate the situation is, how unpredictable the situation is, how the pattern of change is developing, and how much the audience understands about the situation. Let's take them one at a time.

1. Increasing Dramatic Stakes

One way you get the load-bearing pillars of your plot to become higher is by increasing the *dramatic stakes*, which are what will be gained or lost in the encounter with change.

Dramatic stakes can be positive, such as gaining money, as in *The Great Train Robbery*, gaining love, as in *Say Anything*, or gaining freedom, as in *Desperately Seeking Susan*. Dramatic stakes can also be negative, as in *Cliffhanger*, where people will lose their lives if they fail; while in *The Terminator*, the entire human race could be destroyed if the challenge is not successfully met.

2. Increasing Jeopardy

You can also achieve added height by increasing the *jeopardy*, as in Steven Spielberg's television movie *Duel*, in which a small incident on a desert highway eventually becomes a life-and-death battle.

It's important to remember that all jeopardy doesn't have to be physical; emotional violence can be equally gripping, as seen in films like *The Barretts of Wimpole Street* or *Gaslight*. For example, in *The Hand That Rocks the Cradle*, a nanny bent on revenge against the young mother starts by causing intensifying emotional assaults before her attacks turn physical.

Another way you can increase jeopardy is by revealing that the source of opposition is more powerful than originally thought, as in *All the President's Men*, *Witness*, *Robocop*, *JFK*, *The Last Boy Scout*, and *Chinatown*.

3. Increasing Obstacles

You can also add height to story pillars by adding to the *obstacles* that threaten to prevent successful encounters with change.

One way to build pillar height is to increase the numbers of obstacles, as in *Night of the Living Dead* or *The Birds*. Comedies use a similar dynamic with multitudes of small problems compounding the main problem, as in *The Out-of-Towners*, *Bringing Up Baby*, and *The In-Laws*. Another variation occurs when the sources of danger continue to escalate no matter what is done; *The Year of the Comet* used this device.

4. Increasing Desperation

You can add pillar height by increasing the urgency of the situation. This is often referred to as a "ticking clock," meaning that the situation will definitely get worse with time.

One variation is to make sure the audience knows that time is running out, as in *The Andromeda Strain*. Other variations include the declining strength of the hero, as in *The Shootist*, or increasing proximity of danger, as in *The Eye of the Needle*, or declining resources, like running out of water in Alfred Hitchcock's *Lifeboat*.

Increasing desperation can also be created by *shutting doors*, in which possible solutions are eliminated one by one. This technique was used in *High Noon*, whereby various groups of people whom the sheriff thought would support him failed to do so.

5. Increasing Unpredictability

Plot twists are another way to add height to the pillars of your roller coaster. Plot twists are load-bearing pillars which make it seem that a successful encounter with change is impossible. Just as a real roller coaster has both actual and kinetic energies, where riders stop moving forward but feel as though they are still moving ahead, plot twists provide an exciting sensation for viewers. They are key moments of change where the direction or speed of your roller coaster suddenly shifts.

Among the types of plot twists are *barriers*, which occur when the solution a character was counting on is suddenly shut off, as in *Alien*. A *discovery* is a piece of information that changes the significance of previous information, while a *reversal* is when the audience learns that their previous assumption is the exact opposite of the truth, as in *Mortal Thoughts*, or *The Conversation*, in which the young lovers who seem to be the victims are revealed to be the killers.

When using plot twists, it's important to ask yourself what expectations you must create in the audience's mind in order to get the full dramatic power out of your plot twists. Such changes have to be well integrated into the rest of the story, or the audience will feel manipulated or cheated.

6. Increasing Likelihood of Change

Another way to increase pillar height is through a sense of "implied build," which means that the audience, consciously or subconsciously, begins to sense a pattern of difficulties that suggests that the pattern will continue.

Some effective patterns are "quicksand," in which the troubles become more and more enveloping, as in *Double Indemnity*, *Body Heat*, *Dog Day Afternoon*, or the comedy *What About Bob?* "Step by step" occurs when the audience can see a pattern but the character isn't yet fully aware, as in *Reds*, *Green Card*, or *Witness*. Tracking the cumulative changes in such films provides a lot of emotional power even though the individual incidents may seem small.

7. Increasing Revelations

The more the audience understands about the possible ramifications, the more emotional impact the event can have on viewers. Therefore, another important technique to build pillar height is often not to make the series of events on screen more intense, but simply to increase the significance of the information that the audience already has about the event.

For example, a frightened woman sitting alone in a room may not seem too dramatic, so often writers will try to make the scene more dramatic by having the woman shriek in panic or show some other intense reaction. However, such techniques can quickly become melodramatic. Instead, make sure that the audience fully understands the implications of what's happening, then they will supply all the drama that is needed just by exercising their imaginations. For example, if the audience learns that the woman's husband is a killer who intends to murder her, the same scene of her sitting alone in a room immediately becomes more powerful, and when she hears his key in the door, the emotional impact becomes even more intense.

▪ Arranging Your Pillars ▪

Once you are clear on what your key pillars are, you need to start thinking about how to arrange them. You must align them, both in terms of the internal logic of the story line and the emotional height. For example, you may have a clear sense that your character has a major argument with a neighbor, but you need to decide whether that argument should be before or after the character's other argument with the mailman, depending on which scene is more intense.

You won't be able to set these in stone until other creative decisions are also made, but as you think about the plot, keep in mind the image of growing pillars. If you isolate each pillar in your mind and try various arrangements, chances are that you will have a clear visceral sense of which pillar is higher.

Another way to think of these load-bearing pillars is as *landmarks of change*. By tracking them the audience can understand both the pressures toward change, and how far those pressures have advanced in your plotline.

The total pattern of load-bearing pillars, or landmarks of change, should combine to create an increasingly difficult obstacle course. As you continue to develop your plot, you should achieve real clarity about what kind of obstacle course your plotline offers, and exactly what traits it is most designed to test, because that will have tremendous impact on how you will develop your characters.

▪ Designing Dips ▪

Just because the overall pattern of pillars must get higher and higher doesn't mean that each pillar must. As we've discussed before, you can design any kind of roller coaster you want, as long as you are in control of where and how the highs and lows take place.

An intentional dip can be very effective emotionally. For example, the "Columbo" series has used this structure for years. The first spike represents the murder that the audience watches in the first act; then the tension temporarily subsides as Columbo makes his entrance, then begins to build again.

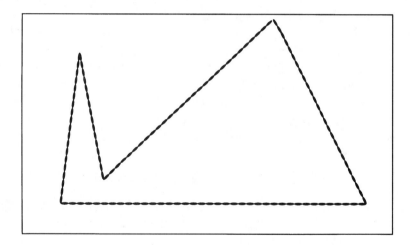

While some films, such as *The Day of the Jackal*, create an almost linear ascending structure, the audience generally needs resting places to catch their breath or get oriented before the next change occurs. Short scenes of comic relief or quiet time can fulfill this function; in fact, horror films often use quiet moments between attacks in order to make the upward surge of audience energy more exciting by contrast.

▪ The Connection Between Plot and Structure ▪

As you continue developing your plot, you will see that the pattern created by connecting the top of your various story pillars reflects the structure. Since the height of these pillars is determined by the intensity of the audience's emotional reaction to various pieces of story information, you, as the writer, arrange those pillars according to your best guess as to how the audience will react. The height you choose for your pillars is a statement—your opinion—of their relative value.

Additionally, just as the top line of your story pillars becomes your structure, the sequence of the story pillars on the bottom line becomes the logical progression of the plot. Therefore, having some sense of the overall structure you are trying to create with your plot is very useful once you identify the emotional pattern you are trying to achieve.

For instance, if you were trying to build your roller coaster with a "big bang" opening, the height of the first story pillar would be the audience's reaction perhaps to a vicious murder, an exciting car chase, a plane crash, or whatever story event is most suitable to your individual story line.

This visual image can be a tremendously useful tool for a writer because it gives you a tangible gauge by which to measure your story. It's not enough to ask yourself, "Which event occurs next?" You should also ask, "How high does the pillar need to be?" and/or "How can I dramatize that event in such a way that it achieves the height I need?" The trick is to make sure that each significant story pillar gets higher, and that the overall pattern is in keeping with your visceral sense of what the structure should be.

▪ A Word About Subplots ▪

As the name implies, a secondary plot is not essential to the story, but it offers the audience additional information about the central events, explaining or illuminating factors that affect the main story line.

Sometimes subplots do this by contrasting with the main story, or sometimes by enriching the main plot by examining motives and decisions. It's important to make a firm decision about what your plotline is and what is secondary. Otherwise, the result can be that issues affecting the central dilemma are left out or underdramatized, while secondary concerns suddenly get far too much screen time.

Subplots should contain a starting point, a pivotal moment of change, and an end result, but do not have as many landmarks of change, and therefore do not demand as much screen time as a main plot. Your subplot is created by story pillars, which should be integrated into your overall roller-coaster design, but they are rarely load-bearing pillars unless the story information is also a key moment in the main plotline.

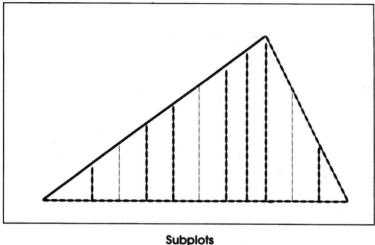

Subplots

You should arrange your subplot story pillars in terms of chronology, logic, and pillar height. For example, you don't want a subplot peaking too soon; it makes the main plot look anticlimactic, which is what almost happened in *An Officer and a Gentleman*. So try switching these story pillars around to make sure they are integrated into your overall roller coaster in the most effective way.

However, plot is not the only ingredient in a successful screenplay, no matter how inventive and exciting. So in the next chapter, let's begin looking at characters to see how that dynamic fits into the mix.

Plot: Building Your Roller Coaster

QUESTIONS

1. What type of change are you writing about?
   Internal?
   Interpersonal?
   Societal?
   Situational?
2. How does it relate to your dramatic center?
3. How does that relate to your overall structure?
4. Do you have a clear sense of the overall roller coaster you are trying to build?
5. How does your plot provide conflict resolution?
   Help viewers bond to the story?
   Supply new information?
   Provide a sense of completion?
6. What is the pivotal moment of change?
   End result?
   Starting point?
   Landmarks of change?
7. What is your dramatic equation?
8. What are the load-bearing pillars?
9. How do you increase the height of your pillars?
   Increasing dramatic stakes?
   Increasing obstacles?
   Increasing desperation?
   Increasing likelihood of change?
   Increasing knowledge?
10. What kind of obstacle course is your plot creating?

EIGHT

Characters: Getting the Audience On Board

Now you've designed your roller coaster and built the pillars to support it. However, in order for it to create a compelling experience, you must get people on board. Luring the audience onto your story roller coaster is the function of characters, which they fulfill by expressing emotions that provoke a sense of recognition in viewers.

The resulting connection between the story and the audience is created through the use of *universal emotions*, the primal, almost archetypal sensations at the root of any emotional experience. For example, the feeling of "not enough" is the same sensation at its core whether it's not having enough money to buy food when you're hungry or a tycoon not having enough to save his vast business empire.

If audiences were only able to relate to specifics of a plot, they would be interested solely in stories that duplicated their own lives. However, through the recognition of universal emotions, which serve as a common denominator between the events in a story and the experiences of the audience, viewers can relate to a character's dilemma using their own experiences as a point of reference.

The audience hooks up with your story through the characters mainly because characters address the four basic audience needs. Universal emotions allow the audience to *bond* with the story, which is the preeminent emotional need addressed by characters. Characters also address the audience's need for *new information* through unusual personalities, habits, attitudes, or philosophies, such as Peter Sellers's character in *Being There*, or Robin Williams in "Mork and Mindy." Audiences satisfy their need for *conflict resolution* by observing how characters deal with their problems. Characters also address the need for *completion*, which is why creating emotional arcs that make sense and move convincingly from beginning to end is so important to an audience's overall satisfaction with a story.

There are three categories of characters—heroes, antagonists, and secondary characters. Each provokes a different dynamic in the audience and fulfills a different function within the story's dramatic equation, so let's look at each in detail. Heroes will be examined in this chapter; antagonists and secondary characters will follow in the next.

Heroes

Heroes are an expression of, and feed the hunger for, the highest aspirations of human nature. Heroes are also an antidote to the audience's sense of daily frustration. Viewers get a vicarious thrill out of watching the hero say and do things that people are reluctant to do in real life.

Audiences are fascinated by how or why people change, so they want role models of wisdom and courage. Whether courage is tested in a big action-adventure like *Cliffhanger* or in a quiet moment of truth as in *Ordinary People*, viewers find watching someone try to "take the high road" inspirational, even when that effort fails. Since one definition of courage is the ability to accept the truth about change and to act appropriately, the two most important criteria for heroes are that they must know, or learn, the truth, and then they must act appropriately.

Sometimes heroes express their truths physically, as Sigourney Weaver does in *Alien*. Sometimes they express themselves verbally, as Peter Finch does in *Network* or as Robin Williams does in *Good Morning, Vietnam*. Sometimes they act with great reluctance, as in *The Quiet Man*, and sometimes with zeal, as in *Norma Rae*. But whatever form it takes, a hero must act by the end of the story. ("Action" can also mean the decisive failure to act. For example, in *Three Sisters* the lead characters talk about change but never take action; their lack of action is every bit as dramatic as any action could be.)

▪ Rooting Interest ▪

Audiences will enjoy a story more if they actually have an emotional stake in the outcome. Effective heroes generate a strong sense of *rooting interest*, meaning that the audience cares greatly about what happens to them and whether or not they achieve their goals.

Similar to the audience at a racetrack, they will enjoy the race and get much more emotionally involved if they have money riding on who wins. It's a feeling of personalized investment, as though viewers have chosen the hero as their horse. The result is that if the hero wins, the viewers win.

Developing rooting interest depends on three dynamics:

1. The audience must want the hero to win,
2. They must think the hero is capable of winning, and
3. They must believe the hero deserves to win.

Many writers interpret the first criterion as making the hero likable. However, that's not inclusive enough because it is possible to develop rooting interest for characters the audience doesn't like. The only real necessity is that the audience must feel empathy with the character, making a connection with the motives, methods, feelings, and/or situation.

The second consideration for developing rooting interest is that the audience must believe that heroes are capable of winning. To put it another way, the audience simply will not bond with a hero they suspect has no chance of success. As in real life, people are protective of their emotions (especially if those emotions could be powerful and sad), so audiences won't bond with a hero unless there is a reasonable chance of an uplifting experience.

For rooting interest to form, audiences should think the hero deserves to win. Consequently, somewhere in the story, the hero needs to demonstrate at least one characteristic that provides a legitimate reason for admiration. That development usually occurs when the hero acts in some way that genuinely impresses the audience, and it is that transcendence of normal inhibition that often defines the hero.

It is a mistake to think that a hero is created or defined by eventual success in the game. Real heroism comes from being willing and able to go into battle; winning the battle, although preferable, especially once the audience has bonded with the character and developed rooting interest, is only a preference. It's entirely possible to be a compelling hero and still lose the final fight, as in a film like *Serpico*.

▪ Matchup of Hero and Obstacle Course ▪

Many writers think that the excitement in a story comes directly from the obstacles in the plot or the compelling personality of the hero, but the real excitement is created by the *matchup* between the hero and the obstacles the hero encounters attempting to reach the goal. For example, crossing a street before the light changes doesn't seem like much of a challenge, especially if the hero is an Olympic runner. However, change the hero to a physically disabled five-year-old boy determined to get across the street without taking his mother's hand, and suddenly the same challenge is riveting.

All the criteria for rooting interest are profoundly affected by the matchup between the hero and the obstacle course. The matchup depends on two factors—the absolute difficulty of the challenge and the hero's relative level of ability. Therefore it is critical that you understand your hero's basic level of ability. The challenge in your story has to be appropriate to the character's abilities; any contest that is too easy or too hard will destroy the balance and tension needed to create a compelling story.

Understanding each hero's level of ability can help you define what each hero needs to do to earn the audience's respect. It will also help you understand their character arcs, the core of their emotional appeal, and how to use your screen time to give the audience the kind of information they need for the character arcs to be most effective.

▪ Four Types of Heroes ▪

There are four types of heroes, all of whom are defined by their level of ability. These categories are not meant to be absolute, but to help you clearly identify and create the dynamics needed to make an audience genuinely root for your hero. Each hero type is life-affirming in the sensations they provoke in viewers. Each type of character helps the audience bond to the story in a different way, and each contributes to a different kind of roller-coaster design.

1. The Idol Hero

An *idol hero* is someone whose level of skills and ability is higher than the average person's. If the squiggly line in the graph below represents everyday life, such as paying bills, driving to work, and minor squabbles, then the idol hero lives and functions on a level much higher.

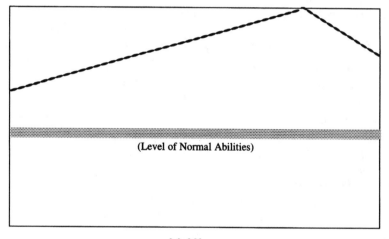

(Level of Normal Abilities)

Idol Hero

As seen through the audience's eyes, the idol hero is someone to look up to. If the audience were schoolchildren, then the idol hero is the favorite teacher, adored and worshipped for being able to handle a situation better than the viewer ever could.

The idol hero takes actions that are not only appropriate, but often inspired. Much of the appeal is that this hero exhibits surprising knowledge and inventiveness. Some examples are James Bond, Hercule Poirot, Miss Marple, and Sherlock Holmes.

Idol heroes usually know the truth right away, have no doubts about their assessment, and take action without hesitation. The defining characteristic is that they have no ambivalence and no self-doubt.

Needless to say, that is very different from what most people experience in their daily lives, so bonding with such heroes, if only for a few hours, provides a vacation from their inner turmoil and confusion. The audience doesn't identify with idol heroes as much as they recognize their own fantasies. There is an exciting, the-sky's-the-limit quality about these heroes.

Because idol heroes have skills and abilities much higher than the average person's, the obstacles they face must be harder than everyday challenges for the central matchup to succeed. This kind of hero demands big-scale conflict, although with some idol heroes—for instance, Sherlock Holmes—the conflict does not have to be physical.

Idol heroes do not undergo major emotional arcs because they begin and end as heroes. Therefore, they work well in stories concerned with outer conflict and change. These heroes act on behalf of justice, usually have a purpose beyond an immediate goal and are faithful in the service to which they are committed. Idol heroes are a driving force because they decide to be one.

Idol heroes can have endearing imperfections, such as Superman's bashful behavior or Sherlock Holmes's social dependence on Dr. Watson, but such decorative characteristics cannot be allowed to detract from their ability to use their skills with strength and precision. In fact, it is a big mistake with an idol hero to focus on ambiguity and doubt; a James Bond who agonizes over every action loses his appeal, because it is primarily his confidence that makes the character attractive and fun.

2. The Everyman Hero

Unlike the idol hero whose abilities and exploits are far above the average person's, the *Everyman hero* exists right in the thick of those everyday challenges.

If the audience were schoolchildren, this hero would be in the same class. As seen through the audience's eyes, these heroes are friends, peers, equals. The same things that are hard for the audience are hard for this hero, and so there is a sense of camaraderie. They go into a challenge with the skills that most people would bring to the situation and are as stumped facing the quandary of the human condition as the viewer.

Some examples of these heroes can be seen in *Hannah and Her Sisters*, *Kramer vs. Kramer*, *Fried Green Tomatoes*, *Poltergeist*, *North by Northwest*, "Roseanne," "Northern Exposure," *Play Misty for Me*, and *Presumed Innocent*.

The Everyman hero provokes a bond with viewers through recognition of

Characters: Getting the Audience On Board

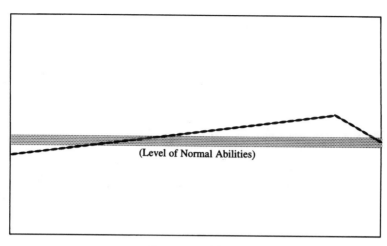

Everyman Hero

and identification with the challenges such characters face. Everyman heroes are life-affirming, because they convey the message that a person doesn't have to be perfect, or brilliant, to succeed.

The Everyman hero can find it very difficult to face the need to accept change and/or act on it. Often the challenges within the story reveal the truth to this hero, and a large part of the heroism is finding a way to accept it, despite the inconvenience, pain, and difficult change it may demand.

These heroes usually have many doubts, and the search for the truth about feelings or situations can take up much of the story. They become heroes only when they are able to rise above the doubt and confusion to act. The audience will be patient as long as they believe (1) the inner conflict is real, (2) the search for the truth is genuinely difficult, (3) the hero is really trying, and (4) the hero will take action once the truth is learned. (However, if the character takes a long time to find the truth and then stalls before taking action, the audience will feel cheated because the character failed to act heroically.)

Bonding with the Everyman hero gives the audience a chance to affirm and synchronize their emotions, as discussed in Chapter Two. These heroes live in a world of doubt, confusion, and ambiguity, and their story is their struggle to rise above that. As a result, their heroism comes from overcoming internal issues in order to influence the outside world. This type of story reflects an obstacle course that forces the hero to rise above natural limits.

Most genre pieces (such as cop, detective, or horror films, Westerns, and love stories) have Everyman heroes because they are the easiest hero to bond with, if well drawn. Alfred Hitchcock, in fact, made a career of what has been described as "ordinary people in extraordinary situations." Despite their many flaws and weaknesses, Everyman heroes are able to rise above those limitations, at least for a moment, to take control of the situation. Like the grandmother who somehow finds the strength to lift the car off her trapped grandchild, these heroes have moments of glorious triumph, although they don't live their lives in such a state. The audience is fascinated by the mechanics of real heroism, which has been defined as ". . . not the absence of fear, but acting despite the fear."

These heroes change through the story, usually because they learn a lesson. Often they start out thinking better of themselves than they deserve; if there is a discrepancy between what the character thinks and does, it is more common that they overestimate themselves. For example, in *Kramer vs. Kramer*, Dustin Hoffman's character thinks he's a swell father and husband at the beginning of the story; it's only through the flow of events that he comes to reevaluate, becoming a hero because he is willing to act on the truths he discovers.

These heroes tend to become a driving force in the story because of their own need for resolution. Since their heroism is defined by facing and accepting the truth despite the pain, it is crucial that the audience have a clear understanding of how much pain they are feeling, and what acting on their truths may cost. *Die Hard* is an excellent example of an Everyman hero; Bruce Willis manages to overcome seemingly impossible odds, but along the way, the audience sees his pain and fear.

3. The Underdog Hero

Underdog heroes are characters at a genuine disadvantage when compared to the world around them. In an objective statement of fact, this kind of hero is not the equal of members of the audience; in some way, underdog heroes lack what the average person has, which prevents them from being successful. Their handicaps can be physical, emotional, social, or mental and must be legitimate, in their own estimation as well as the audience's.

If the audience were composed of schoolchildren, this type of hero would be the little kid who wants to walk with them to school but can't keep up.

Underdogs become heroes by triumphing over obstacles in order to take control of their lives. Some examples are *Rocky*, *Gaslight*, *Raising Arizona*, *The Elephant Man*, *The Jerk*, *King Kong*, *An Officer and a Gentleman*, and *Lorenzo's Oil*.

These heroes often know the truth early, and their heroism comes from sticking to that truth even when the appropriate action is hard. An example would be stroke victims who know they want to walk again; their heroism comes from their repeated efforts to succeed, despite all obstacles.

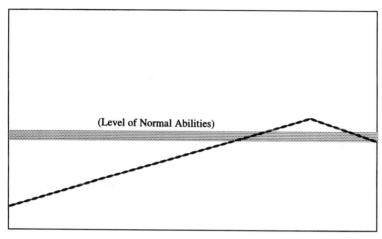

(Level of Normal Abilities)

Underdog Hero

These heroes have great ambiguity, and generally underestimate themselves. Part of their potential for heroism is that they are much more capable of change than they realize. Underdogs can start out as losers, but there must be some indication to the audience that the underdogs can win, even if they don't believe it themselves. Planting seeds of greatness in the characterization of an underdog is important because the audience will not bond with a weak character with no chance of winning. The underdog must have potential to win, even if the circumstances and odds are against it.

Everyone knows how hard it is to stay on a diet, or save money, or stand up to the boss, so it's easy to admire a character who overcomes even greater challenges, like a stroke. The example of courage despite overwhelming odds is what makes the underdog hero life-affirming to the audience. Screen time spent ensuring the audience knows the handicap is real and the odds are overwhelming will heighten these stories' appeal. It's also important to emphasize the underdog hero's tenacity and discipline because it makes the accomplishments even more impressive.

These heroes change over the course of a story, especially in their view of themselves. In fact, if there is a discrepancy between how they see themselves and how the world sees them, they think more poorly of themselves, in the beginning, than others do. These heroes, therefore, are usually involved in transformation stories. Underdog heroes gain new ability, or new understanding of their ability, through the obstacle course of the story.

These heroes usually know what they want early in the story, but have to find the strength to achieve it or even to believe that it is possible. Their goal is usually expressed in an external challenge, such as learning to walk again after the stroke, but the more difficult challenge is the conquest of their internal doubts, discouragement, and fears.

As a result, underdogs become heroes when they conquer their internal obstacles long enough to overcome external obstacles. They are not usually a driving force in the story until pushed to be by outside circumstances, as in *Karate Kid*; they finally change because they are unwilling to endure any longer the pain of remaining the same.

4. The Lost Soul Hero

The heroes we have discussed so far create a bond with the audience through positive emotions, but the *lost soul hero* expresses the darker side of human nature, an aspect of the audience's life they rarely want to talk about or deal with. If the audience were schoolkids, the lost soul would be the kid who defies the teacher but later doesn't have the good sense to buckle down, and so, ultimately, gets kicked out of school.

Some examples of lost soul heroes appear in *Bonnie and Clyde, Amadeus, Thelma and Louise, The Executioner's Song, Sugarland Express, Raging Bull, Midnight Cowboy, The Conversation, Citizen Kane,* and *Dracula.*

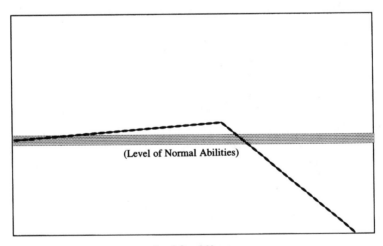

(Level of Normal Abilities)

Lost Soul Hero

From the audience's point of view, this is a peer who takes the wrong turn, goes down the wrong path—"There but for the grace of God go I." Viewers are intrigued by this glimpse of the "dark side."

This kind of hero avoids knowing the truth, fails to act on it, or takes inappropriate actions. To form a bond the audience needs to empathize with the hero's motives, at least in the beginning. Audiences can admire the precision of their actions or the intelligence of their plans, such as in *The Day of the Jackal* or *The Godfather*. Viewers can sympathize with their lack of options, as in *The Executioner's Song*. In a strange way, viewers can even admire the courage it takes to be bad, since most people are reluctant to pay the social and internal price of being bad in real life. In order to pursue their paths, lost soul heroes often have to break out of the mold, resist peer pressure, and stand up to internal fear or their own conscience.

Audiences admire these heroes' courage to be bad because most people have longings to do bad things. They are not stopped by personal morality, but by fear of the consequences. Because those consequences hold most people in check, audiences are fascinated by someone who isn't stopped or made hesitant by those same forces.

This kind of hero is life-affirming. Initially, the audience has the guilty feeling that they, too, would make the same choices when the crimes aren't too bad; after all, it's fun to have the dark side released temporarily. Eventually, though, the hero goes one step too far, and the audience pulls back; they experience a sense of relief and personal encouragement that they are not bad after all; they feel they have better moral or ethical judgment than the character; indeed, in their negative space, the audience feels superior.

The last scene in *The Godfather* is a perfect example of this dynamic. When Michael Corleone chooses to lie to his wife, it signals his complete reversal of the values that he held at the beginning of the story. As the camera pulls back, leaving him to face the future he has chosen alone, the visual image represents the same dynamic that is occurring in the audience's minds.

The final rejection of the lost soul's actions and values, when viewers abandon the lost soul to the dark path chosen as they return to the light, is what makes this hero dramatic. Because of the previously established bond between these heroes and the audience, viewers have a sense of loss or mourning as they leave these heroes to face their bleak fate alone.

These heroes change as the story progresses, but always in a downward direction. Often they have a chance to learn a moral lesson that could save them (and secondary characters in such stories often learn that lesson and pull out in time), but these heroes don't learn it; the audience does, however, which confirms the value of existence.

Individually, this hero's decisions and actions must make sense, or seem acceptable at first (*My Brother's Keeper*, for example), but slowly the character's path begins to go astray. These heroes' ultimate desires may not be admirable,

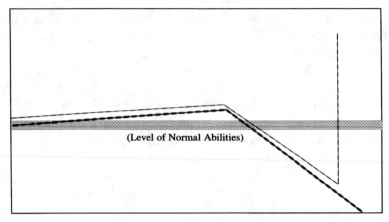

(Level of Normal Abilities)

Audience Reaction to Lost Soul

but they must be understandable, because if the audience can't imagine wanting the same things, viewers' eventual rejection of this character will reflect much less courage on the audience's part and be less intense and emotionally satisfying at the end.

▪ Which Hero Is Right for Your Story? ▪

Determining which hero is right for your story depends on what your dramatic center is. What kind of change do you want to dramatize? What kind of roller coaster are you trying to build? A story about small, incremental changes may need an underdog hero, while a story about big-scale action battles may demand an idol hero.

The level of ability of the hero is also a crucial factor in expressing the dramatic equation of your story. How strong are the forces of good? How tough is the challenge? If you have a clear sense of the statement your story is conveying, it will help you determine how strong the hero should be and what kind of strengths your hero should have. You must become very conscious about what kind of hero you are creating and why that hero is ideally suited to the obstacle course of your plot so that you can use your screen time to communicate that information to viewers.

▪ Making Your Hero More Effective ▪

Here are some techniques for making your hero more effective:

1. Separate the Hero from "the World"

The hero should always be in contrast to, if not actively in conflict with, the "world" of the story. It is that separation that makes his or her story worth telling. For example, an advertising executive who loves his work, gets along with everyone, and has no complaints about the company is not as innately interesting to write about as an executive who hates working there, participates in office gossip, and plots his escape.

The issue that separates the hero from the world is also crucial to your story because it is a tangible expression of the dramatic center of your script. For example, in my Lizzie play, it was her inability or unwillingness to be repressed any longer which eventually separated her from her world. Sometimes heroes are fully aware of these differences from the beginning of the story, as in *One Flew Over the Cuckoo's Nest*, while other heroes do not realize that crucial difference until the climactic moments of the story.

Sometimes this dynamic is referred to as the "fish out of water" genre. Any story benefits from some element of polarity because it implies an inevitability of conflict that is structured into the central logic of the story. Some scripts really focus on that difference, and others use it more for texture, but any story is strengthened by the polarity because that ability to hold to one's beliefs despite peer pressure is really the essence of heroism. The more the element of separation is explored, the stronger the hero will seem.

You can intensify the audience's awareness of this polarity by your choice of *story arena*. Ask yourself how much you want to draw attention to the contrast, and then what arena would reflect the appropriate contrast. For example, the hero of *Working Girl* was made more effective because the people of her world did not support her aspirations. Similarly, *Beverly Hills Cop* was made more effective by placing Eddie Murphy in a posh setting; in his own world he still would have seemed like a nice guy, but since his values were in keeping with that world, he would have seemed much less special.

2. Establish a Personalized Link Between Hero and Audience

"Make your hero likable." In some ways this advice makes sense; if characters are likable, they are more pleasant to spend time with. However, this rule is not absolute and can be quite limiting and incomplete, especially for lost soul heroes.

Another conventional wisdom is that you must create sympathy for the character, but, again, it's only a good technique for some types of heroes; it significantly undercuts the appeal of an idol hero, for instance.

Instead you must focus on making your hero *empathetic*, so that viewers feel a sense of recognition and affinity on some level. In fact, an unsympathetic character whose feelings the audience understands is much more powerful than a sympathetic character whose stick-figure emotions are too generic to seem believable.

3. Establish the Hero's Strengths

Rooting interest should build over time as the audience learns about the characters. While the hero submits to pressure or deals with increasingly difficult circumstances, more and more admirable qualities about him should become evident to the audience. As the obstacles get more and more serious, the audience must develop more reasons to have confidence in the hero, or the hero will soon seem unequal to the challenge. If the audience were allowed to know everything right away, the characters would fail to perform their main function—that of luring the audience onto the roller coaster and keeping them enthralled.

As a result, it is essential that heroes have at least one strength, a secret weapon, that spark of convincing heroism which is the reason they will win if they win. That information can be obvious, as in idol heroes, or conveyed in subtle "seeds of greatness" for an underdog, but regardless of how you address this in your script, it is central: the audience won't bond with heroes unless they have a credible chance of success.

4. Establish the Hero's Vulnerability

A hero doesn't have to be perfect. In fact, except for an idol hero, heroes need something to overcome or they won't seem heroic. It adds to the excitement of your story if there are real doubts about the hero's strengths, just as long as those vulnerabilities don't contradict the hero's essential appeal.

What is your hero's secret liability, the reason the hero will lose if the hero loses? The secret flaw—the Achilles' heel—is crucial to developing a well-rounded character. As you develop the central matchup, think about the events of your plotline and why they would have greater impact on your hero than on someone else. For example, in *Agoraphobia*, the hero was phobic about spiders, which makes the dramatic stakes go up significantly.

5. Define the Hero's Values

Values are usually what separate the hero from the world, although sometimes heroes don't know it at the beginning of the story, as in *Norma Rae*. Such values are connected to your dramatic center and are also a crucial element in the creation of the dramatic equation of your story.

6. Establish the Hero's Motives

In order for the audience to empathize with the hero, they must understand the hero's reasoning and private emotional desires and not just the external action chosen to achieve the outcome. Such motives are often connected to the dramatic stakes of your story and can either be positive ("I want to make more money") or negative ("I want to avoid being poor").

7. Establish the Hero's Goal

The hero's goal is always to complete the obstacle course successfully, but exactly what that means may not always be evident at the beginning of the story. Sometimes the obstacle course is apparent from the beginning of the script, as in *An Officer and a Gentleman*; sometimes the obstacle course emerges or becomes more difficult unexpectedly, as in *The Out-of-Towners*.

8. Establish the Hero's Plan

Understanding the hero's plan gives the audience the ability to measure success or failure, gain or loss, along the way. As with the hero's goal, the plan may be evident early in the story, as in *The Great Train Robbery*, or becomes so as the story progresses, as in *Lorenzo's Oil*.

9. Pearl of Battle

In a well-constructed story, the pivotal moment of change often forces heroes to reveal their true nature—not what they think they are or what the world thinks they are or what they want the world to think they are—but what they are in their essence. That is the moment of truth. Usually that quality of truth would never have been revealed except by the struggle, and so it is the *pearl of battle*, a moment of beauty created by irritation and difficulty.

QUESTIONS

These categories are not meant to be absolute; rather, they are meant to start you thinking about your hero's level of ability so that you can make certain your hero will be well challenged by the events of your plot.

Characters: Getting the Audience On Board

1. What kind of hero is best suited to your story?
   Idol?
   Everyman?
   Underdog?
   Lost soul?
   Why?
2. What kind of change are you trying to dramatize?
3. What qualities do you need to spend your screen time establishing in order for the audience to bond with your hero?
4. What are the universal emotions that the audience can relate to in the hero's dilemma?
   How do you intend to show them?
5. Is there a good matchup between the hero and the obstacle course?
   What makes it an exciting contest?
   Why are this hero's strengths and weaknesses the best matchup for that obstacle course?
6. What kinds of skills does the hero have?
   Does the hero have seeds of greatness?
   An Achilles' heel?
   A clear motive?
   A goal?
   A plan?
7. What separates the hero and the world?
   What makes the hero distinctive?
   Sets the hero apart?
8. What are the values the hero holds?
   How and/or why do they set the hero apart?
   Does the hero hold them at the beginning of the story?
9. Does your hero evolve from beginning to end?
   If so, why? How?
10. How does your hero address the need for new information?
    Bonding?
    Conflict resolution?
    Completion?
11. How does the hero rise (or fail to rise) to the occasion?
    What is the "pearl of battle"?
12. Have you safeguarded the core of your hero's appeal?

NINE

Creating Other Characters

We've seen how heroes fulfill their function of luring people onto a story roller coaster by expressing the desire for a positive encounter with change. However, not every human emotion is lofty, nor every desire pure. Other types of characters are needed besides heroes. Through these other characters, viewers are drawn on board by giving them a chance to express and explore their negative emotions, their deepest fears, darkest angers, and most morbid fantasies. Allowing the audience to vent such sensations is the function of *antagonists*, who represent the destructive side of human nature.

Secondary characters are also important in fleshing out the dramatic equation of your story as you focus on separating the hero and the world. Having characters who function as friends, confidants, supporters, and auxiliaries makes it easier for the audience to develop an emotional connection to both the positive and negative dynamics that are playing themselves out in the dramatic equation of your story.

Creating Other Characters

Antagonists

A well-known industry saw claims that "Good villains make good movies." Creating a compelling film is not quite that simple, but it is true that many stories get their theatricality and power from the villain, the "bad guy," the renegade who is often more dangerous and more intriguing than many mainstream heroes.

While everyone can relate to the dreams and desires expressed by a hero character, having those desires thwarted is perhaps an even more universal experience. As a result, antagonists express the viewer's fear, frustration, and even nightmares, representing the forces of opposition.

Not every story needs to include a human antagonist. *The Old Man and the Sea* is an example of this; others include *Being There*, *Citizen Kane*, and *Diner*. In fact, many films involving internal conflict, or with lost soul heroes at the center, have no need for an antagonist, because the heroes contain the seeds of possible destruction within themselves.

However, most stories benefit from having a personalized focus of opposition. They provide antagonism, resistance, or the contrary force that often creates an active battle between good and bad, right and wrong, productive and destructive.

Even if your story deals with internal or situational change, the more external action and confrontation you use, the easier it will be for an audience to become involved with the story. Societal conflict must be made personal by inept officials as in *The China Syndrome*, or situational by the reactions of different people to the same crisis as in *Jurassic Park*.

And in *Amadeus*, a brilliant examination of inner turmoil, the conflict and change facing Salieri were easier for the audience to grasp by placing Mozart in opposition. In reality, Mozart didn't cause Salieri's confusion, nor was there a struggle between the two men. Rather, the cause of the problem was Salieri's own inability to make peace with himself, a very personal (internal) struggle. Through Mozart's presence, Salieri—and the audience—became more conscious of Salieri's deficiencies and his corresponding discomfort with them.

▪ The Matchup of the Antagonist and the Hero ▪

In many ways, heroes are defined by the opposition and can only be as interesting, compelling, or exciting as the forces they are up against. Antagonists are the representation of the forces that oppose the hero and thus the audience, so they must be as overwhelming as possible, because that is how people perceive their own problems.

The relative strength of the hero and the villain is also an important aspect of your dramatic equation. The more powerful the antagonist, the stronger your hero will seem; in fact, a powerful antagonist gives a film much of its emotional impact, because it determines the difficulty of the challenge to which the hero must rise. There is no suspense if the hero and the antagonist are not well matched.

▪ The Three Kinds of Antagonists ▪

Just as heroes are defined by courage, antagonists are defined by how powerful they are, and how much they enjoy being destructive.

1. The Fiend

As seen through audience's eyes, the *fiend antagonist* is more than their equal. Matching the idol hero in ability, the fiend's skill level is very high, if not superhuman. The fiend is similar to the idol hero in many ways, yet because of different moral values, the fiend serves destruction while the hero tries to build or preserve.

The essence of fiends is that they are not stopped by the things that stop "normal" people, such as inner morality or social limits, which the average person acknowledges and accepts. In fact, they actually enjoy destruction, whether it's to guarantee their own survival, as in *Dracula*, or for entertainment, as in *Batman Returns*. In comedies, much of the humor comes from their lack of sensitivity to the usual social norms.

Fiends are most effective when powerful, theatrical, evil, and extreme. Some classic examples are Freddie of the *Elm Street* movies, Dr. Moriarity in the Sherlock Holmes films, and Darth Vader in the *Star Wars* epics. Other examples are the shark in *Jaws*, the car in *Christine*, and Glenn Close in *Fatal Attraction*, with comic examples that include Bill Murray in *What About Bob?* and the father in *Life with Father*.

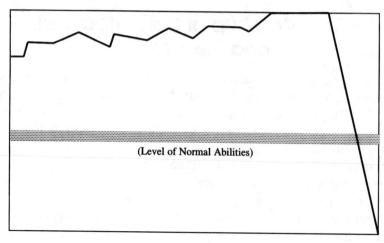

Fiend

When the battle is idol vs. fiend, there generally are large-scale events and major stakes, as in *Terminator 2* or *Goldfinger*. A fiend against an Everyman makes for an exciting contest, because it is very clear from the beginning that the hero is outmatched. That type of contest often forces heroes to rise above natural limits, at least for a few moments. The suspense about whether they will be able to transcend their limitations is exciting. The Everyman becomes a genuine hero, triumphing over the odds. *Die Hard*, *The Eye of the Needle*, and *The Silence of the Lambs* offer examples of this matchup, and most horror films tend to be in this genre.

You don't often see a fiend against an underdog. The hero is so outmatched that the contest is hard to sustain. However, you can see this in some subplots, as in *The Wizard of Oz*, or with the cruel nanny against the mentally disabled gardener in *The Hand That Rocks the Cradle*.

2. The Adversary

Adversaries function at the same level of ability as Everyman, and are not necessarily evil; they just have a different agenda. As seen through the audience's eyes, these characters are the audience's equal in abilities and often attitudes, and are often normal people—even good people—whose desires are in conflict with the hero's. Often these antagonists don't intend to destroy, even though that is the result of their actions.

An adversary against an idol is usually an unequal match unless there is a group of adversaries involved. *Robocop*, for example, pitted a bunch of adversaries against an idol hero. An adversary against Everyman tends to explore the more complex issues of the human condition, where there is no automatic

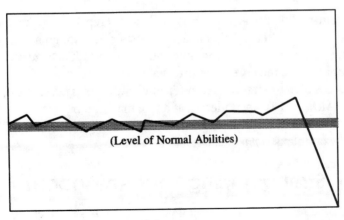

(Level of Normal Abilities)

Adversary

right or wrong. It is also common in genre films, like Westerns, detective stories, cop films, and love stories. Some examples are *North by Northwest* and *Kramer vs. Kramer*. An adversary against an underdog is often a comic device, as in *No Time for Sergeants*, *The Pink Panther*, or *Home Alone*.

3. The Pest

The *pest* kind of antagonist is not the audience's equal in innate power or personal ability. Pests tend to get their power from their position, which they often misuse. Because of the low level of ability, this character is often seen in comedies, and is the least frequent type of antagonist because the ineptitude prevents the central matchup from being exciting.

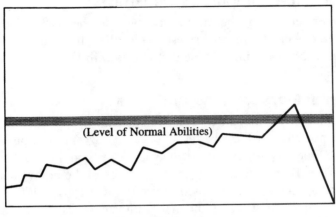

(Level of Normal Abilities)

Pest

Pest against idol: Because there is such a discrepancy in their levels of ability, you do not often see this matchup sustained through an entire story. However, you can see a partial example with the kids in *Kindergarten Cop*. Pest vs. Everyman is the most frequent use of a pest antagonist, because it reflects the audience's own frustrations. Some examples are *Ferris Bueller's Day Off* and *Dennis the Menace*. Pest vs. underdog is a rare matchup because the pest, who functions as an irritant, often seems petty against a legitimate underdog, but one good example is *Home Alone*.

▪ Strengthening Your Antagonist ▪

Here are some techniques for making your antagonists more effective:

1. Make Them a Representative of the "World"

Just as the hero is strengthened by being separated from the world, the antagonist's power base comes from the fact that the world of the story often supports the antagonist's basic values, even if the antagonist later takes those values to an extreme.

2. Establish the Antagonist's Strengths

It can be quite effective to give the antagonists at least one likable, even admirable, quality, because that prevents the audience from dismissing them at once as utter bad guys. These "seeds of greatness" can make the antagonist's eventual loss or defeat more provocative, and this is particularly true in the contest between adversaries and Everyman heroes, which can provide a forum for exploring issues of deeper emotional complexity.

3. Establish the Antagonist's Weakness

As with your hero, giving the antagonist an Achilles' heel can add excitement and unpredictability to the contest, especially when the antagonist is a fiend. Otherwise, it can seem implausible that heroes with lower levels of abilities would be able to win.

4. Establish Motives, Plans, and Goals

Often people feel that they are up against an unknown, or at least an unnamed source of opposition, so it can be very effective to stagger revelations about the antagonist. One way is to reveal the antagonist's methods but not the motivation, as in *Die Hard*. Another possibility is to reveal the motive but not the identity for a while, as in the discovery of the bad cops in *Witness*. Either device can help create suspense and make ultimate revelations more effective.

Creating Other Characters

Additionally, knowing an antagonist's goals and plans gives the audience a way to measure the character's success or failure at any point in the story. A clever and complex plan can also add to the audience's sense of the antagonist's power.

Secondary Characters

Secondary characters give depth, explanations, and richness to the main story. Often the plot is concerned with just the skeletal actions; secondary characters are a chance for the audience to learn the details. Plot may be confined to the external actions the hero takes, while the motivation has to do with inner drives and is connected to dramatic center.

The function of secondary characters is to explain, examine, and heighten contrast between the hero and the world. Scenes with confidants, friends, lovers, supporters, mentors, and advisers allow a hero to express thoughts, desires, goals, plans, and values. They are characters used to define the hero and the hero's world, people who really explain who the hero is and why. Secondary characters can also be used to examine the world of the story, including the antagonist's character, values, and world view, thus intensifying the polarity between the hero and the world. The more you define one, the more you imply the conflict with the other. It makes the hero more distinctive by contrast and makes the obstacles against him more formidable.

For example, in *Escape from Alcatraz*, every scene, subplot, and secondary character that helps convey Clint Eastwood's character's concern for humanity gives the audience a deep visceral sense of his values, while every scene that shows his world, including the secondary characters of the guards, the huge slamming steel doors echoing in the hard stone halls, and the rigid regulations, conveys a sense of why there will be an inevitable conflict between the hero and the world.

Therefore, once you have chosen an *arena* for your story that amplifies the difference between the hero and the world, you need to populate both sides of that dramatic equation. You need to show the audience the people and events that explain and magnify the contrast of the two world views. Such divisions are an integral part of your dramatic equation, heightening the audience's sensitivity to the values and conflicts involved.

Important though they may be, make sure your secondary characters don't overshadow your hero and antagonist. This problem occurs frequently because secondary characters aren't the writer's alter egos (as the hero or antagonist is) and therefore seem easier to write.

Fleshing Out Characterizations

Characterization is giving the audience the pertinent information to assess the characters' strengths and weaknesses, and why they are so well suited to battle. In general, the depth of your characters equals the emotional depth of your exploration into the human condition.

Some characters' emotional reactions to change are very complex—as Al Pacino's character in *Scent of a Woman*—but not all scripts need in-depth characters. In fact, many high-concept films are marketable largely because audiences don't need to know a great deal about the characters' personalities in order to predict what kind of roller-coaster ride it's going to be. You don't need to know much about the woman's personality in *The Terminator* to imagine the terror she feels being chased by an indestructible monster. However, even mainstream commercial films like *Lethal Weapon* are strengthened by compelling characters, and soft-concept films like *Driving Miss Daisy*, *On Golden Pond*, or *Fried Green Tomatoes* will live or die on the strength of personalities.

1. Clarify the Character Arc

A *character arc* is the character's emotional reaction to the sequence of events which are your plot. For example, the plot of *Becoming Colette* details the husband's manipulations of his young wife; her reactions, which take her from an innocent country girl to a renowned writer, are her emotional arc.

In order for character arcs to be successful, the audience must understand who the characters were in the initial status quo, who they are at the end of the story, and why each emotional change in between led to the next. It also helps if the audience understands what forces are causing the change, what forces are making it difficult to deal with the change, and what the character's step-by-step reaction to each key moment is.

Some key moments for heroes or antagonists are the starting point, landmarks of change, the pivotal moment of change, and the end result. Character arcs can focus on in-depth emotional changes, or simply adjustments of problem-solving strategies, but it is important that there be new stages of difficulty and reactions to those difficulties in order to create enough new information to keep your audience interested.

2. Focus Your Characterizations on the Present Tense

I often meet writers who put all their energy into figuring out the back-story, or personal history, of a character. They then spend a great deal of screen time on the resulting details, yet as the character proceeds throughout the story, it becomes clear that the details are irrelevant. They have not affected the character's actions or motives in any way.

Rather than providing back-story, I urge you to focus your imagination on the actions, characteristics, language, and behavior that can make the character interesting in the current story. What determines whether a character is successful is how well that character evokes the audience's interest in the present tense. People develop strong, clear impressions about other humans based solely on present-tense body language, word choice, and general behavior without really knowing much about their back-stories at all.

Think about it: Don't you have firm impressions and opinions about your neighbors, co-workers, and many other people you pass in the course of the day even though you actually know little or nothing about their backgrounds? That's because the way someone speaks, moves, and looks gives you strong ideas of those people, and it is these qualities that are essential in establishing a characterization. The audience will only be curious about someone's back-story if there is something about their present-tense behavior that makes them curious.

3. Use Back-Story Only if It's a Revelation

Writers should focus on the provocative and unique elements of a character's behavior in the present. Back-story is only valuable if it surprises the audience or explains why a person is acting in a curious manner. It's only interesting if it makes them act differently in the present or contradicts the audience's impressions of them.

For example, if a female character seems sophisticated and elegant, perhaps the audience assumes she is from a wealthy urban family. Therefore, if they find out that she's actually from a small farm in North Dakota, it's interesting; it puts a lot of questions in the viewer's negative space: "How did she get from there to here?" "What drove her to change her essential self so much?"

No matter what the questions, however, the longer the audience has held that impression of the character, the more interesting such surprises will be. Therefore, it's a good idea to hold surprising revelations until later in the story. In the above example, information given to the reader on page fifty, after the audience has developed its own expectations of the character, could be intriguing. Give the reader that same information on page three, however, and it might be mildly interesting, but have none of the power of the later revelation.

A rule of thumb: Don't use exposition unless it's going to change the audience's opinion of the character.

4. Avoid Decorative Tags

Don't focus your creative energy only on coming up with imaginative eccentricities, or *decorative tags*, for characters. It may or may not be helpful to know the character has some endearing trait, and that fact may or may not increase the effectiveness of the story. Instead, what the audience must know about characters is how they will function in the matchup. Therefore it is the information about the strengths and weaknesses that prove pertinent to the central contest that is vital for the audience to know.

Decide on and convey the information that explains why the central matchup is exciting. Don't get attached to lots of details about your characters unless it affects the core dramatic questions of your story; focus on strengths and weaknesses of character that are pertinent to your central story.

5. What Is Your Character's Self-Assessment?

Sometimes a hero thinks he is one thing and the audience thinks he is another; for example, in *The Pink Panther*, the hero thinks he's an idol while the audience perceives him as an underdog. Fiends can think they are adversaries, or even think they are idols. Such miscalculations can be tragic or comic, but when they exist, it's important information for the audience to know.

6. Show, Don't Tell

Don't just tell the audience that the hero is likable or the antagonist is a fiend, make the audience feel that way towards them. You must provoke the emotions in viewers so that they experience the power of your dramatic equation viscerally. After all, the story experience that matters is the one which happens inside viewers' heads.

7. Don't Underestimate the Power of "Small Moments"

A *small moment* occurs when genuinely revealing data is disclosed but the character thinks the world isn't watching. In a small moment, the character makes no effort to put on a "mask," thereby allowing the audience to glimpse the "real" person. This is how the audience experiences their own lives, so small moments help in the process.

A great example of small moments was in *Dances with Wolves* when Kevin Costner's character was alone in the fort. If those moments had been edited out of the movie, the overall plot would not have changed, but the audience's sense of bonding to the character would have been significantly diminished. Not only would that have lessened the overall enjoyment of the film, but it could also have weakened the second half since the audience entered the Native American's foreign culture feeling very bonded with him. Without that closeness, the audience might have found it harder to relate to his acceptance of the tribe.

Small moments don't change the overall direction of the plot; however, they are absolutely crucial for creating a strong character bonding. The power of small moments comes from the fact that characters have let down their guard. They give the audience more intimate knowledge of what the character is really like. More scripts fail due to lack of small moments than big moments. Small moments help the audience to bond to the characters; without that bonding the audience doesn't care about what happens to the character.

QUESTIONS

1. Is there an antagonist in your story?
2. If so, what kind of antagonist is best suited to your story?
   Fiend?
   Adversary?
   Pest?
3. What is the core opposition between the hero and his world?
4. What is the world's value system?
5. How is that opposition dramatized, presented, personalized?
6. What is the core opposition between the hero and his world?
   What are the *values* of that world?
   What is the source of power?
   What type of logic dominates?
7. Are you using your secondary characters to *illuminate the values* of either the hero or the world?
8. What are your hero's small moments?
9. How does your hero feel about himself?
   Where is the character's self-investment? What is the hero proud of?
10. What are the character's decorative tags?
    How do they connect with the central challenge?

Momentum: Building Your Engine

*I*magine that you've designed your roller coaster, built the pillars to support it, lured people into the cars, and then—nothing happens. No ride, no movement, nothing. That's what occurs when a roller coaster doesn't have an engine, and the same thing happens to an audience's interest if a story roller coaster doesn't propel them forward. Thus the next major element in building a story roller coaster is *momentum*, the energy that drives the audience's emotional and logical processes forward to completion.

Momentum is a crucial element in a successful story roller coaster, yet it is one of the least-addressed topics in screenwriting. When discussed at all, one theory claims that it's created by the hero's desire for a goal. However, there are many compelling films like *The Graduate*, *Kramer vs. Kramer*, and *The Burning Bed* in which heroes don't know what they want until far into the story, so what provides the momentum then? Another theory equates momentum with pacing, suggesting that a story will hold the audience's interest as long as actions, words, and images move quickly. However, speed is not enough to guarantee audience interest; for instance, several of my friends thought the final segment of *2001: A Space Odyssey* was agonizingly slow, despite the fact that the visual images moved at lightning speed. The problem was they had no emotional or intellectual interest in that segment of the story.

So what is momentum? Momentum is the audience's hunger to know what's going to happen next. That eagerness for information is not a passive state of mind, nor is it one that you can assume viewers will achieve by default. It's all too easy to "zone out" in front of the television or be distracted in a movie theater. When that happens, the audience's negative space is dominating their awareness, so their minds are filled with such thoughts as how they're going to pay their bills or how annoying the sound of popcorn crunching can be. What you want instead is for the positive space of your story to dominate their awareness. You want them totally absorbed in your story in both an intellectual and emotional quest to find out what's going to happen. If you can get your audience involved in trying to find the answers to the questions that have formed in their minds, then that effort becomes part of their story experience, shrinking any distracting awareness of their negative space and enlarging their involvement in your story. That is the energy needed to create the sensation of a compelling, fast-moving roller-coaster ride.

Asking and Answering Questions

The energy to process a story is the result of *questions* forming in the audience's negative space in reaction to story information. The audience members ask themselves questions in order to get oriented, work their way through a myriad of information, and figure out what's important and what's not.

The first questions the audience usually ask are ones that help them get oriented in the story, so during the first few minutes, the internal dialogue is often "Who is that guy?" "Is that his sister?" or "Why are they fighting?" As the story progresses, the questions then focus on the emotional and logical ramifications of change, the importance of the change, or the characters' reaction to change. Those questions often boil down to "Why?" or "How?"

Momentum: Building Your Engine

This is such an automatic process that it's virtually impossible to have the viewers *not* ask questions.

"Why" questions tend to focus on the motive of a character or the logic of the plot progression, and the essential "Why" question is "Why now?" Some examples are "Why is he leaving the marriage now?" or "Why did she say that now?" "How" questions focus on the process of emotional or logical problem solving, and the essential question is "How will that intention get accomplished?" Examples would be "How are they going to escape past the guard?" or "How will they meet the deadline?"

Additionally, the audience will not only have questions, but their minds will attempt to provide possible answers as well. Consider your own mental process next time you go to a film. After you ask yourself questions, you will begin to guess the answers, which means evaluating the story material for possible clues. If the movie stopped halfway through and someone asked you to articulate your reasoning, you might be surprised to see just how thorough and detailed it was.

Audiences not only try to guess the right answers, but one of the reasons they stay with a story is to see if they are right. It's almost as though the story becomes a game in which they bet on the outcome and therefore have something at stake.

Audiences don't want their guesses to be completely right, of course. In fact, it's very disappointing if they are able to determine easily how a story's going to resolve. It makes them feel as though the game was not worth playing and that the storyteller let them down. On the other hand, they also don't want the final answers to be so obscure that the solution is impossible to find; that also makes the game worthless, because there is no chance of winning.

What viewers want is something in the middle. When the solution is revealed, they want to realize that the story gave them enough clues to find the answer, but that the storyteller was clever enough to distract them from the clues' real significance. The resulting feeling is that they lost fairly, a very important criterion if the audience is to find a story emotionally satisfying.

Evidenced by this active question-and-answer process, every story is a mystery to viewers, regardless of its genre. As a story progresses, the audience should develop both logical questions and emotional concerns that they are eager to have answered, because it is the intensity of their interest which creates the feeling of momentum.

Making sure that viewers have enough information to get emotionally involved without making the story predictable demands very careful storytelling and is something that you shouldn't even worry about in first drafts. But as you begin to polish your screenplay, you must pay close attention to this dynamic, because a story roller coaster will not create a compelling ride without strong momentum, no matter how interesting the other components are.

How Momentum Addresses Audience Needs

Momentum's primary function is to fulfill the audience's emotional need for *completion*, and every aspect of the intellectual and emotional energy employed in the question-and-answer process is the result of the audience's hunger for closure. Momentum can also address their hunger for *new information*. Because the very process of trying to find the answers to their internal questions forces the audience to constantly process clues, even familiar material can seem new in context. The audience's need for *conflict resolution* is addressed as they imagine various scenarios and evaluate whether each one will solve the issues in the story, and *bonding* occurs when they become totally absorbed in these efforts.

However, none of these needs can be successfully met if the screenplay fails to provide viewers with a strong sense of *author credibility*. The audience is continuously evaluating whether the effort to find answers is worthwhile. If the audience doubts that the storyteller will eventually answer their questions, they will withdraw from the process, killing momentum entirely. The audience will not commit themselves to playing the question/answer game if they don't think it's possible to win, or at least learn the answers.

Creating Questions

One way to ensure author credibility is by planting in the audience's mind the questions that you intend to answer. Any questions will create at least short-term interest, but because of the intensity of the activity in the audience's negative space, it is very important that you, as the writer, consciously create questions in the audience's mind that will focus their attention on the aspects of the story that you want to be prominent in their negative space.

To create questions in the audience's mind, you "black out" moments, deliberately omitting information that they need to understand fully the changes in your story. It's almost as though you line up all the scenes that will be necessary to tell your entire story, and then decide which ones you'll black out, thereby focusing the audience's attention on the conspicuously missing information.

An obvious example of blacked-out information occurred in the "Mission: Impossible" series. In each episode the audience was allowed to see the portion of the scene in which team members were given their special tools and disguises, but they were not allowed to see the portion of the scene in which their use was explained. This led to the viewing audience questioning how the devices would eventually be used, as well as to an exciting sense of discovery when the answers were eventually revealed.

Blacked-out information is central to your story dynamics; with this omitted information, you intentionally focus the audience's interest on an event or piece of information, then leave it out. The audience will register an implied question in their negative space and begin looking for the answer, which contributes to the sense of momentum in your story.

Curiosity and Suspense

There are two states of mind that can be created by the decision to black out some story clues. They are *curiosity* and *suspense*. Both are valuable for creating and sustaining audience interest and forward momentum.

Take sports. If people watching a football game only know the most basic rules, they will probably lose interest quickly because they know what's happening but they don't understand its significance. In contrast, if they know all the rules, have extensive knowledge of the teams, believe the teams are evenly matched, and have a strong preference as to which team will win, they will watch the same game with a passionate level of interest because they understand the significance of the possible outcomes; they just don't know which will occur.

Curiosity is equivalent to the lower level of interest in the football game. It occurs when viewers know what events are happening, but they don't know why. Curiosity is easy to create, because all that is needed is a moment when there is a discrepancy between the events in a story and the audience's expectations of the norm. Such expectations may be created by previously established story information or simply the norms of everyday life. For example, if a character were established as easy-going and good-natured, then suddenly began a tirade for no apparent reason, there would be a story-based discrepancy. By the same token, even in the first scenes of a script if an ordinary-looking woman suddenly shrieks in panic after seeing a red hat on the ground, the audience would also recognize a discrepancy, even before they have any idea of the woman's specific personality. Once viewers sense a discrepancy, the question that automatically springs to their mind is "Why?"

If you want to create curiosity, you will give the audience full information about the immediate events, but you will black out the explanation. For example, in the opening sequence of the film *Shoot to Kill*, the audience sees a pajama-clad man frantically using keys to open the thick glass door of a commercial establishment. Moments later he is in a jewelry store, where he hurriedly throws diamonds into a container, while carelessly dropping many on the floor. Within seconds, the audience is curious: What's going on here? The normal expectation is that burglars are much more deliberate and not usually dressed in pajamas, so viewers' minds immediately start piecing together the available information hoping to discover an explanation that makes sense.

Because curiosity can be created so quickly, it is very useful in overcoming resistance at the beginning of the story. Curiosity engages the audience because they begin forming questions in their negative space. But since curiosity is based on an active sense of disorientation, the audience can soon become uncomfortable with their lack of knowledge, and that sense of discomfort increases over time. That sense of conscious dissatisfaction disrupts their concentration and therefore hurts the sense of momentum, so once you intentionally plant curiosity in the viewers' minds, you need to understand that the "meter is running." You must give them an answer, or some hint that you will eventually answer their question, or you risk hurting your author credibility.

Additionally, since curiosity depends on a lack of clear orientation about the significance of events, prolonged curiosity weakens the audience's ability to bond with a story and can eventually result in confusion, impatience, or even anger.

Thus a better storytelling technique is to provoke initial curiosity, then build on that interest by turning curiosity into suspense. Suspense is similar to the second level of interest in our football analogy, and it occurs when the audience understands the significance of possible outcomes, but doesn't know which one will occur.

To create suspense, you must give the audience all necessary information about the possible ramification of outcomes, but black out the knowledge of which one will occur. Using the *Shoot to Kill* example, the suspense begins once the audience understands that the man is the owner of a swank jewelry store and his wife has been kidnapped; his carelessness is due to his frantic distress in trying to comply with the ransom demands. What they don't know now is if he will succeed.

Suspense is most successful when the audience also has developed an emotional bond with the characters, and because suspense is based on a stronger level of audience orientation than curiosity, it can be maintained for longer stretches of time. However, due to the audience's emotional involvement and conscious concern for the characters, an active sense of suspense can become increasingly unpleasant for viewers, so one of the reasons suspense generates strong momentum is that the audience eagerly searches for an answer in order to bring the unpleasant sensation to an end. In fact, if suspense goes on too long without any promise of relief, viewers will begin to resist the continued unpleasantness, which disrupts their concentration and works against the sense of momentum you are trying to build.

A film doesn't have to be a thriller or a horror film to use suspense. In fact, virtually every successful story eventually creates that sensation, because it is the natural result of the viewers' mental processes when they are in a state of expectation—a state of eagerly trying to guess what will happen next—which is exactly what you are trying to generate in your audience's minds. To ensure the sense of expectation needed to create either curiosity or suspense, you must generate a combination of direction, doubt, and desire within your viewers' negative space.

Momentum: Building Your Engine

Direction

The first thing an audience needs in order to develop expectations, and therefore a strong sense of momentum, is a sense of *direction* about where the story is going.

In order to feel a basic sense of direction, viewers must have some idea of who the main characters are, what the hero wants to achieve, what the obstacles are, what kind of matchup exists between the hero and the challenge, what is at stake, and at least some indication of how they are supposed to feel about the story. The audience doesn't need to know all of this immediately, but they do need a sense that the storyteller knows and is prepared to let them in on it at some point.

Creating a sense of direction is important because until viewers are given enough information to make some assessment of the situation, it is difficult for them to develop expectations, or try to guess the answers to their questions, or even know what questions to ask. That confusion will make them more aware of their negative space than the story events in the positive space and thus weaken any chance of forward momentum.

The need for direction is particularly strong in the beginning of the story, because the audience cannot assess whether later information is pertinent until they have a sense of what the story is about. The sense of direction is usually established in the form of a *story click*, which is when the audience gets an initial sense of what kind of story it's going to be. It is the "Oh, I get it" moment. This moment usually occurs when the audience understands that the hero's encounter with change has begun. For example, in *Chinatown*, the story click is when Jack Nicholson learns that he has been tricked into taking the case by the encounter with Faye Dunaway; in *The Verdict*, it is the moment when Paul Newman rejects the settlement and decides to take the case to court.

Some writers think of the story click as the "inciting incident." However, that label focuses your attention on the internal logic of a story, while the real importance of a story click is as the key moment of orientation for the audience. The quicker the audience is given enough information to assess the starting point, the more clearly they can process the significance of the changes in the story.

This does not have to be done in the first ten pages, as conventional wisdom suggests, but you should be conscious of the fact that the audience will not totally relax until they have this information. They won't feel comfortable until they have some sense of direction because they don't know where to focus their attention or what criteria to use to process and evaluate the on-going story information.

Many writers are reluctant to give viewers too much information because they are concerned that the audience will become bored. Ironically, it is the lack of direction that is alienating to viewers. So don't be too subtle in your presentation of the story click, because viewers are actively looking for that sense of "you are here" on the map of the story.

Another way to give an audience a sense of direction without telling them too much is by using setups and payoffs. A *setup* is a nugget of story informa-tion that will answer the audience's questions later on. Setups hint at what people, events, and issues will be central to the story, thus giving the audience a sense of direction. Setups are a promise that the author makes to the viewers, and the *payoff* is the moment when that promise is fulfilled. As more setups occur, the trail of nuggets gradually leads viewers through your story, creating momentum through the sense of direction which develops as the clues accumulate, and allowing viewers to develop expectations that they become increasingly eager to see are correct.

There are two kinds of setups, conspicuous and inconspicuous. Fore-shadowing is a conspicuous setup, an intentionally theatrical hint that viewers should pay attention to some aspect of the story. The audience experiences setups as the storyteller points to a nugget of information and says, "Pick this up; it will come in handy." The audience puts it in their mental knapsack and carries it with them as they move into the world of your story. An example of foreshadowing is the use of music that signals the presence of the shark in *Jaws*, or a closeup of a knife which is later revealed to be the murder weapon.

The other kind of setup is planting seeds, which are inconspicuous setups. This kind of setup is not obvious when first introduced but proves useful over time. In fact, part of creating a fun roller-coaster ride for viewers is the sensation created by planted seeds that don't seem important at first but later prove to be exciting and provide unexpected answers to key questions the audience has developed. The writer's challenge in using these setups is to distract viewers from their real importance by focusing the characters' atten-tion, and therefore the audience's, on some secondary concern. In fact, the sense of direction created for the audience by planted-seed setups does not come from their eventual importance, but from the disguise the writer uses to conceal their real significance when they are first introduced.

Momentum: Building Your Engine

For example, in *The Big Easy*, Ellen Barkin makes love with Dennis Quaid, then comes downstairs the next morning and pats him on the rear, only to discover that it's his brother she patted. The focus of that scene is her embarrassment as she quickly leaves the apartment, and the audience's attention is on how passionate, yet tenuous, the relationship between the lovers really is. However, a half hour later in the story, when the brother is shot on the street because he looks like Dennis Quaid, the audience suddenly understands the real significance of the earlier scene.

When used successfully, planted-seed setups add excitement to the rollercoaster ride, because the audience experiences such moments as a "gotcha!" They suggest that viewers should stay on their toes because there could be more surprises along the way, as in films like *Body Heat*, *The Verdict*, and *No Way Out*. Planting seeds can be a very effective storytelling technique and enhances author credibility when well done. In order that it be done well, you have to make sure that the viewers think they fully understand the significance of the planted seed at the outset and don't realize they've been duped until the additional layer of meaning is revealed.

The sensation that the audience experiences when a foreshadowed payoff works well is that the nugget of information they picked up now comes in handy, so they feel clever to have noticed it before and smart to understand how it answers their current questions.

However, the desire for that sensation explains why unanswered setups are so frustrating for viewers. The failure to pay off prevents them from having that complete sense of satisfaction at the end of the story and prevents that sense of completion for which they go to films.

There are a lot of levels on which a story can be satisfying for the audience, but the ability to pick up the necessary clues and then use them later on is a big part of it. In a well-scripted film like *Body Heat*, some of the definite thrill in the final portion of the movie is the fact that all the information we have gathered about the character and the situation comes into play.

Cumulatively these promises add up. Because they linger in the audience's mind, especially when something is set up more than once, you want to use these setups to focus viewers' attention on things that lead to important changes and issues, and you want to make sure that you set up everything you pay off, and vice versa.

Here are some general tips on creating a sense of direction:

1. Only set up what is absolutely necessary.

Because the audience often puts extra energy into picking up all available clues, you should only set up what is absolutely necessary.

2. The more conspicuously something is set up, the bigger the payoff must be.

The longer you conspicuously hide a secret from viewers, the more important it becomes and the more impact it must have when it's revealed. If this doesn't happen the audience will feel a sense of disappointment, and the moment will feel anticlimactic.

In the movie *The Outlaw Josey Wales*, Clint Eastwood spit and spit until I thought it would drive me crazy. It was such a prominent part of his character, I became convinced that it would have a big payoff, like winning a crucial shootout because he was able to spit in someone's eye. However, the payoff came only halfway through the movie, and it wasn't significant, so even though most of that film was brilliant, I was momentarily disappointed because the story failed to pay off what had been set up so successfully.

3. Don't answer questions until the audience "asks."

Don't give the audience answers until you have created curiosity in them about the answer. For example, if you want to tell your character's back-story, make sure that you've created at least one moment of genuine curiosity about it. Then you can tell the viewers. Before you've established that curiosity, the exposition is distracting detail at best because the audience doesn't have a context to hold that information, and so the importance of the details could easily be lost on them. Afterwards, it becomes an exciting revelation, which is much more fun for viewers.

4. Revealing information gradually is more effective than explaining it all at once.

It's very effective to reveal answers gradually, or to reveal only portions of answers and withhold the final details that make it all make sense. That allows viewers to feel confident that you know they are waiting for an answer and intend to tell them at some point. It also lets them know that you are in control, and that they can sit back and trust that they will get all their questions answered eventually.

A good technique to use with exposition is to dole it out in tiny amounts, ideally spreading it throughout the story so that the momentum never stalls.

Stopping for information which doesn't answer the audience's current questions often causes a break in the forward thrust and may even confuse the established sense of direction. This is why many people don't like flashbacks. There's no hard-and-fast rule that says not to use them, but as with all exposition, use them sparingly and carefully or they will cause your roller coaster to slow down.

The gradual "reveals" in a story can really help build pillar height, especially if it's an unraveling of the central questions that have been driving the story. You can also disguise exposition by incorporating it within a bigger emotional moment. It could be during a fight, as comic relief, whatever, but, much like planted seeds, if you focus the character's attention within the scene on something else, the audience will also be distracted successfully.

5. Don't tell the audience too much too soon.

An example of "too much too soon" for me was the first scene in *The Big Easy*. I was figuring out the "headlines" (he's a cop, that guy's dead, it's night, they're talking with a Southern accent) when suddenly the characters launched into a detailed discussion of who the various bad guys might have been. When I first saw the film (much of which I loved, by the way), I was haunted by the fact that I had not understood something important.

The problem was that telling exactly who the bad guys were, down to their nicknames, was far too much detail for me to take in, and at that point, I had no real curiosity about who had killed the person. I was much more interested in finding out who they were, and what was the dead man's relationship to the people on the screen.

6. There is a ratio between how important information is and how quickly it is paid off.

If a setup provides an important piece of story information that significantly changes the status quo of a story, the audience needs some time to adjust before the status quo is changed again, which is the payoff. Thus the ratio between setup and payoff is crucial. If the interval is either too short or too long, the impact of the cause and effect is lessened; the story can lose its forward momentum or even become melodramatic.

7. Pay off everything you set up.

Because of the effort an audience puts into picking up conspicuous setups, unresolved setups are very dissatisfying. Loose ends impair the audience's sense of completion and undercut the story's ultimate impact.

Doubt

Another important element in developing momentum through expectation is *doubt* in the audience's mind about whether the hero can overcome the obstacles. Creating genuine doubt can be very difficult since today's cinematically literate audience is well aware that most Hollywood movies have happy endings. As a result, any script that centers around the question, "Will the hero succeed, yes or no?" is not going to generate much doubt.

However, there are two types of questions that are much harder to guess the answers to and thus are better at creating real doubt. They are "How?" and "Why?" These questions force viewers to get much more specific in their attempts to analyze the situation, thereby creating stronger personalized involvement and more hunger to know the outcome. This state of mind contributes to the sense of momentum.

Since the climax is the moment when the ultimately *how* or *why* question is answered, the decision of which type of story is best suited to your screenplay depends on your dramatic center and your dramatic equation.

Screenplays become "How?" or "Why?" stories once the author decides which type of questions will best focus the audience's attention on the central dynamics of the story. This is particularly true for the pivotal moment of change, when the audience should experience the dramatic center of your story and understand why the dramatic equation plays out as it does. If your dramatic center has to do with motivations, feelings, or emotional realizations, you are probably telling a "Why?" story. (Even stories that initially seem like "Who" stories really don't satisfy the audience until viewers learn "Why" the guilty characters acted as they did.) If your fascination is with the practical, problem-solving techniques and rational judgments, your story is probably a "How?".

As the writer creates a trail of how or why questions for the audience to follow, the audience develops an increasing need to know the ultimate answers, which provides a sense of satisfaction when they are revealed in the end.

You want your audience focusing on the appropriate questions as they proceed through your story because what viewers think about in their negative space will dominate their experience with your story. You want to use momentum to focus the audience's attention on the important issues, thus intensifying the key aspects of your story.

"How?" stories involve the central question of how the hero will win. When it's already clear that the hero will win, "How?" stories are very useful. Rather than focusing the audience's questions on whether the hero will win, which is easily predictable, "How?" stories center suspense on how the hero will achieve the goal. A lot of the excitement in a "How?" story comes from creating audience doubt about success by showing them how powerful the obstacles are, how large, how determined, how resourceful.

"How?" stories are particularly useful with idol heroes, such as James Bond, Sherlock Holms, Perry Mason, or Superman, where there's not a strong sense of suspense about whether the idol hero will succeed. However, if you leave in the scenes where the problems become evident and black out the scenes which convey the hero's strategy, then the question "How will the hero win?" can be quite compelling.

In contrast to the "How will the hero succeed?" stories, "Why?" stories take advantage of the audience's hunger for explanation. These kinds of stories often build towards revelation about motivation, thought process, or emotional priorities. In "Why?" stories, the blacked-out scenes involve why the hero makes the decision. Psychological thrillers tend to be "Why?" stories, as do most true-life crime stories. Many TV movies re-creating crimes leave the final reenactment to the end because that scene answers "Why?" Some examples are *A Kiss Before Dying* and *Fatal Vision*.

A story doesn't have to be fully a why or how story. In fact, often a *why* main plot will be balanced by *how subplots* or vice versa. In such stories, the *how* element addresses the external actions of the plot, while the *why* element addresses character motivation.

Desire

The last crucial ingredient to create expectation, and therefore momentum, is *desire*, which can either be focused on wanting to know what happens to the hero or wanting to know the answer to the dramatic equation.

Ensuring that the audience develops an *emotional need* to stay with the story is one reason why creating rooting interest for the hero is so important. If the story fulfills all three criteria for real rooting interest—that the hero is capable of winning, deserving to win, and strengthened through the conflict—the rooting interest creates both an emotional and logical investment in the hero's victory.

There are several things audiences desire. One is to see heroes triumph over change and to get away with whatever risk they took. That sense of a satisfying ending may mean that the heroes don't have to pay a price, or that the price they pay seems worth it. Even if the hero doesn't succeed in the eyes of the world, the hero should feel that the sacrifice has been worthwhile, as in films like *Serpico* or *High Noon*, since either the world is better because of their sacrifices or they know they did the best they could.

The desire to have their questions answered is also a powerful drive, because audiences want to "make life make sense," to have their questions answered, and to see if their guesses were right. That hunger for completion is a driving energy, and audiences will lose enthusiasm for the story if they don't believe they will eventually learn the answers.

The desire for resolution involves the audience looking for the end result created by your plotline, and it must be very specific to the logical and emotional progression of your story. It is the answer to the dramatic equation for which your audience has been searching. If the resolution does not fit, the ending will seem contrived or anticlimactic. In fact, in a well-constructed story, there will be surprises along the way, but by the time the ending is revealed, there is a sense of inevitability that is justified by the central logic of the story. A large part of your audience satisfaction with a story is whether the dramatic equation has added up to the ending.

The logic for the happy ending or unhappy ending needs to be set up within the story. A forced, contrived happy ending is not satisfying because it is not well justified and does not give the audience the sense of "playing fair" which they desire. It is possible to simply end the story with ambivalence, but you need to be aware that you are working against the audience's innate hunger for resolution, and so you must find some other way to provide a satisfying sense of closure.

All these desires also play into the deeper, more profound hunger of the audience to know the answer to the dramatic equation. In that sense, the entire story becomes one big question, and the *answer* (the outcome which completes the story's statement) involves both the experience of the dramatic center as well as the outcome of the plot.

The sense of denouement, or the slowing of momentum, occurs most successfully when the audience's desire to know the answers to key questions has been sated, which allows them to begin an emotional tapering-off period. As a result, it's a good idea to keep the final resolution as short as possible. It's as though there's only a little screen time for the audience to regain their composure, to come back up to the real world without getting the bends.

Now that we understand how a story's logical forward momentum affects the audience's emotional reaction, let's examine the impact of style, which intensifies the emotional impact of your story dynamics in order to underscore its dramatic equation and its logical sense.

QUESTIONS

1. What do you want the audience wondering about?
2. How does that connect to the dramatic center of your story?
3. How does it affect the dramatic equation of your story?
4. Is it a "How?" or a "Why?" story?
   What are the central *how* or *why* questions?
   Does it advance the heroes' inner motivation?
   Outer goal?
   Are there subplots that answer the other questions?
5. Is anything set up?
   Foreshadowed or planted seeds?
6. Is everything set up paid off?
7. When do you use curiosity?
   Suspense?
8. How do you provide direction for viewers?
   Provoke doubt?
   Ensure desire?

ELEVEN

Style: Greasing the Tracks

N ow your roller coaster is built, people are on board, and the engine is ready to go. However, to make sure your roller coaster provides the compelling ride it was designed to deliver, you must make sure that every inch of your track is as polished as possible. Otherwise, the disruption created by jolts and halts and snags and jerks can weaken the appeal of even the best-designed ride.

Thus the last major element in building a story roller coaster is *style*, the imaginative restatement of the major dynamics of your story integrated into every layer of the script. It should be evident in the plot, characters, momentum devices, visual effects, narrative techniques, and any other component you use to tell your story.

"Style is the feather in the arrow, not the feather in the cap," a great quote by George Sampson of Cambridge University, really says it all, because style, if well used, helps your script soar and can give it intensity, unity, and focus. The peripheral messages conveyed by the constant and consistent use of style do not contribute just to the audience's logical understanding of the story, but to their visceral understanding of the dramatic equation as well, leading them to experience the dramatic center.

Style works as an intensifier so that viewers can experience the world of the story in a more subjective and intense way. It helps create an all-enveloping sensory experience that heightens the audience's reaction, sending them the key signals of your story on both the conscious and subconscious levels.

In order for your story to be the most effective, you must take viewers beyond their conscious assessment of your story, beyond logic and weighing of facts. Yet the process of presenting story information is rarely evocative enough to create resonance, especially when your story is still on the page.

That is exactly when careful use of style can be so effective. It is the very peripheral nature of style that makes it so powerful; it appeals to the audience on a deep, nonverbal level. By surrounding viewers with color, rhythms, language, movement, settings, and sounds, all of which combine to create a unified visceral sensation, you can reach them in a primal, nonintellectualized way. Its impact is related to behavioral psychology: If you fill the screen with harsh, gloomy colors and slow, plodding music, you can create appropriate emotions in your audience more easily than if you simply fill it with people who are talking about their depression and anger in a beautiful garden on a cheerfully sunny day.

Imaginative, well-used, stylistic choices create a three-dimensional quality in character, place, time, and the world of the story which allows a reader to experience your script completely, transcending the logical, cause-and-effect information contained in the basic plot. When successfully used, it will also help suggest images to executives, directors, and producers that are vivid and evocative, making it easier for them to "see" a script in their minds, helping to convince them that it will make a great film.

Audiences go to films for an experience, for sensation. They want to feel sated, inundated, which is why films that generate strong emotional impact are usually the big hits. It is usually style, carefully orchestrated to intensify the logical and emotional elements of the story, that contributes most to impact.

Style: Greasing the Tracks

How Does It Feel . . . ?

Stories are most effective when they answer the audience's hunger to know "*How does it feel to . . . ?*" and style is the most effective way to transcend a one-dimensional, intellectualized appreciation and create an all-enveloping sensual experience to answer that question in a visceral and immediate way. "How does it feel to die of cancer?" "How does it feel to win the lottery?" "How does it feel to climb Mt. Fuji?" are variations of the essential desire audiences go to films to fulfill.

That's because an effective answer to "How does it feel to . . ." addresses all four of the audience's primal needs at once. It addresses the need for *new information* by answering their curiosity about "How does it feel to . . ." be an astronaut or sail around the world—without having to take the risks. When this kind of story is effective, it is one of the most thrilling sensations, a way to experience how other people's lives feel, to see how other people live, and experience a new point of view.

The audience *bonds* with the story and the characters, because style helps them imagine the world of the characters and to see it through their eyes; in fact, the more subjectively that information and sensations can be conveyed to viewers, the more immediate an impact it will have, and it's the peripheral, emotion-based style choices that enhance the sense of subjectivity. In answering "How does it feel to . . . ?", you don't just tell us how the character feels, but ideally you make the audience feel it as well.

A good example of this was evident in *Ghost*. The moment Patrick Swayze was shot, there was a flurry of quick cuts, startling images, and shocking juxtapositions. For a moment, viewers didn't know what was happening, which was exactly the sensation the character was also experiencing. As a result, the film didn't just *tell* viewers he was scared and disoriented, it made the audience *feel* it the same way.

Conflict resolution also ties into "How does it feel to . . ." You can intensify the audience's understanding of the hero's fear of change, the power of the opposition, and the matchup between the hero and the obstacle course through creative style choices. A good example is *Throw Mama from the Train*, in which the physical attributes of the actress who played the mother, the use of extreme closeups and other subjective intensifiers, really made the audience understand both Danny DeVito's and Billy Crystal's dilemma.

"How does it feel to . . ." also addresses the need for *completion* because style helps provide an all-enveloping sensation of thorough satiation.

Style as Signature

As a result of its peripheral powers, style is a potent tool, and one that conveys individuality and vision faster than any other. It is an opportunity to make a personal statement. Your unique "voice" is comprised of all the stylistic choices that you make. Style can charm, shock, amuse, seduce, intrigue, or startle viewers, all of which can help overcome viewers' initial resistance to a story and provide strong moment-to-moment interest, as well as intensifying the major dynamics of your story.

Think of your favorite filmmakers. Alfred Hitchcock, David Lynch, Steven Spielberg, Martin Scorsese. The first thing that comes to mind is their style. In fact, often a filmmaker isn't really considered a big success *until* the world can see a recognizable style. Oliver Stone was a journeyman writer and director making a living in the field long before he became prominent; it wasn't until the audience began to see a recognizable signature to his work that he really developed into a major presence in the field.

It can be the same with screenwriters.

So few writers consciously and consistently use style throughout their scripts, learning to use it well is a sure way to help your script stand out from the crowd.

▪ How Does This Apply to Writers? ▪

At this point in my class, I am usually asked, "But isn't the style of a film the domain of the director?" And the answer is that to some extent it is. By the time an audience sees a *completed* film they are seeing the results of the other artists' choices made while transferring the story from page to screen.

However, there is a great deal a writer can do on the page to suggest certain tones, pacing, colors, textures, and many other crucial signals to the reader that can create vivid impressions of the world you are writing about. So it is crucial that you make active and consistent choices and incorporate them into your screenplay so that you don't abdicate in this vital area.

We will discuss the techniques for writing evocative stage directions that convey a vivid visual and auditory sense of style in the next chapter, but first let's focus on how to decide what stylistic elements bring your script to life.

The Two Basic Tools of Style

Despite all the millions of distinct and fascinating worlds that film can create on screen, there are actually only two tools that filmmakers—and therefore screenwriters—have at their command: *sight* and *sound*. Everything they try to create and suggest has to be "made" out of something the audience can see and/or something they can hear.

However, through the imaginative use of revealing details, you can create such a rich sense of atmosphere that people can feel almost as though they are experiencing the events with all five senses. In fact, the challenge for the writer is to use visual and auditory clues to go beyond that single sense and suggest images provocative to the other senses, so let's examine the power and use of both.

1. The Visual

We have all heard that "films are a visual medium," but why is that true? The reason is that sight dominates humans' sensory input; in fact, 80 percent of all information about the world around us comes through the eyes. As a result, the communication between the process of visual input and translating that information into meaningful data is finely tuned, and the brain is able to process the information immediately.

For example, if people see a train speeding at them, they understand immediately how far away it is, how dangerous the situation is, whether it is relevant to them or not, and therefore decide quickly how they want to react. All of that information is processed in their brains without having to be verbalized; in fact, it takes more time to express such information in words than to process it internally.

As a result, visual stylistic choices, conveyed in clear, concise stage directions, can quickly create provocative images in the audience's mind, and their emotions will often react instantaneously, allowing your screenplay to take on a vitality and immediacy that significantly heightens its emotional impact.

Your choice of colors, props, actions, gestures, shapes, textures, movement, characters' physical appearance and mannerisms, sets, costumes, actors' appearances, and locations can all convey visual information to readers, even on the printed page. *Batman, Howard's End*, "Miami Vice," "Northern Exposure," *Dracula*, and *Blade Runner* are all examples of films or shows that have a strong visual component.

2. The Auditory

People get only 20 percent of their information in a film from their ears. Not only is sound slower to travel than light, but people process sound more slowly too; there is a slight delay between the time people hear a sound and the time they understand its significance. Yet sound is a potent source of emotion, often overlooked, especially at the script phase.

Sound gets much of its potency from the fact that it can harness people's emotional energy in the very process of trying to understand the location and significance of the source. For example, if you suddenly hear a huge crash while you are reading this book, it would take you a second to understand if it were near or far, human or not, dangerous or irrelevant to you. Until all of those factors are understood, there is a sense of fear, of possible danger because the required gap of time needed to process auditory information leaves humans temporarily vulnerable. In fact, Nietzsche called the ear "the organ of fear."

To completely understand its power, try watching a horror film with no sound, then listening to the sound track of a horror film without the visuals, and see which one is scarier. Sound forces people to get both intellectually and emotionally involved in translating the information. It's the imagination that makes sound so potent, as the people who wrote for radio knew back in the golden age when the "theater of the air" thrived.

However, sound does not have to produce just fear. It can add strong atmosphere, texture, and tension—think of the ticking clock on the mantel, the sirens racing by on the way to a fire, lovers trying to have an intimate discussion on a crowded subway platform. There are many sound applications in film: dialogue, sound effects, silence, volume, frequency, music. It is really limited only by your imagination.

Style Spectrum

Now that you are aware of what tools are available to you, the next decision to make is how intense and conspicuous you want to be in the use of style. Some stylistic choices are very obvious; others are more subtle. How glaring or subtle you are in your stylistic choices will determine where your screenplay falls on the style spectrum.

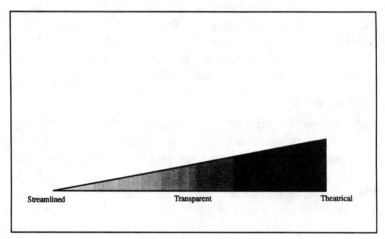

Streamlined   Transparent   Theatrical

Style Spectrum

1. Transparent Style

This kind of style choice is in the middle of the style spectrum and contains nothing conspicuous. It seems to be a realistic portrayal of the world of the film. *Transparent style* seems invisible because it doesn't call attention to itself. But transparent does not mean nonexistent.

In reality there is no such thing as a lack of style, even if there seems to be abdication of it. The writer may well be making subtle choices about colors, styles, and textures that seem so appropriate to the story that they are virtually unnoticeable.

Some examples of effective use of transparent style are *About Last Night, All the President's Men, Tootsie, Fried Green Tomatoes*, and *Howard's End*.

2. Theatrical Style

One extreme of the spectrum is used when recognizable factors of the world we know are evident, then exaggerated. *Blade Runner*, for example, seemed to be a statement of technology gone mad.

Use of this type of high-profile style loses its effectiveness if it becomes unfocused or too cluttered. In my opinion, *The Adventures of Baron Münchhausen* marked such an occurrence. Certainly that was an amazing-looking film and virtually each clip of celluloid was an event, but because it lacked a recognizable truth at the center, I had to get reoriented time and time again, and my dominant impression of the film was a wild visual ride with no emotional center. I'm not saying there wasn't any; Terry Gilliam is a brilliant filmmaker with a very sophisticated view of the world, but I couldn't "get it."

Some examples of effective use of theatrical style are *Batman, The Fisher King, Brazil, Blade Runner*, and *The Addams Family*.

3. Streamlined Style

The other extreme on the spectrum represents style used sparingly. The effectiveness of *streamlined style* depends on choosing just the right "revealing details," because through those you will reveal the meaning of your story. Streamlined style often reminds me of my days in "experimental theater." We hung black drapes at the back of the stage, and all the actors wore black leotards. Then the cowboy wore cowboy boots, the ballerina wore a tutu, etc.

This type of style choice gives emphasis by eliminating clutter and everyday objects, so that the colors or objects left on the screen have added impact.

If you make this style choice, it's very important that you get clarity on what aspects of your story must be emphasized and which can be made secondary. In *Dick Tracy*, the emphasis was on the color scheme, but all other visual elements had simple lines and few distracting details. Often this style tends to be more serious. Many foreign films fall into this category.

Examples of streamlined style include *Closet Land, Interiors, Twelve Angry Men, Our Town, Raise the Red Lantern*, and *Basic Instinct*.

Areas of Style Choices

In addition to the intensity and conspicuous nature of your style choices, you have a variety of categories in which you can make interesting style choices.

1. Color

The *color palette* of a picture conveys a real sense of time and place, even if just mentioned occasionally in stage directions. Think of how important the cold, gray world of *The Addams Family* was to the final picture, the lush colors of *The Last of the Mohicans,* or the richness of the outdoors compared to the more muted tones indoors in *And a River Runs Through It.* Color was also used effectively in *The Wizard of Oz,* which went from black-and-white to full color, and more recently it was used in *Kafka.*

Granted, you cannot capture completely on the printed page the full intensity of these stylistic choices, but carefully chosen stage directions, focusing on the revealing details of color, can plant the right kinds of images in the minds of the reader.

2. Texture

Carefully chosen details cumulatively serve to convey a strong sense of *texture* and can enrich the reader's experience of your script. For example, texture played a big part in conveying the dramatic contrast of the policeman's world and the wealthy woman's in *Someone to Watch Over Me.* Texture is the "adjective" describing your scripts, as in the sultry, steamy sensibility of *Body Heat,* the grimy world of *Midnight Cowboy,* and the oddly sterile fantasy universe of *Edward Scissorhands.*

3. Rhythm

Rhythm is a very potent area of choice because it can be the metronome of the story. Rhythm can be conveyed in dialogue, length of scenes, or speed of events; it can be constant within a script, as in *His Girl Friday,* or it can be used to create bold contrasts, as in *The Godfather,* which juxtaposed slow, quiet scenes showing people's reverence and respect for Marlon Brando's character with fast-paced action sequences illustrating the danger and violence of that world.

One reason rhythm is so potent is explained in a theory that claims rhythms approximate the human heartbeat. If it's a little slower or a little faster, it is within people's psychological "comfort zone," and events that occur within that pace seem "normal" and do not attract attention. However, events that happen faster or slower quickly become conspicuous, and that discrepancy from the norm can be quite effective.

For example, a film like *Barry Lyndon* makes brilliant use of slowness; Kubrick captures the very essence of life in that pre-Industrial time with the dramatically measured pacing that is incorporated into every aspect of the film. The dialogue is long and formal, the costumes heavy, the camera angles just right. It would be possible to cut that film down to a more conventional rhythm by simply editing out the long crosses, the slow scenes, etc., but it would change the film fundamentally. In contrast, a film like the original *His Girl Friday*, the raucous comedy with Cary Grant and Rosalind Russell, captured the vibrancy of the characters, the newspaper business, and one-upmanship of the central relationship by its split-second pacing, overlapping dialogue, and quick, short scenes.

Of course, your entire film doesn't have to be set at one pace. In fact, it is often extremely effective to increase speed to intensify action sequences as the final events of the story play out or slow the pace to make suspense almost unbearable. Other choices will make an important scene linger on the screen, either by elongating it or by playing a key moment in slow motion. Try to use rhythm consciously, imagining that each twist and turn of your roller coaster will be more effective as a result.

4. Duration

Duration is another interesting category of style. How long you take for events to occur in your story, in fact, how long a story you decide to write, can make a significant difference in its emotional impact on the reader or audience.

Take Ken Burns's brilliant *Civil War* shown on PBS; the very pace at which the story unfolded, the actual screen time the audience spent with various characters enhanced the emotional impact of the story. At first the thirteen-hour film may have seemed slow and even a touch repetitive, but by the last night, when viewers finally learned what happened to those people with whom they'd spent so much time, they were deeply and even unexpectedly moved, which proved to be a big part of that film's dramatic impact. Daytime soaps gain lots of their emotional impact simply from the hours spent with these characters. The same is true of a well-structured mini-series.

"Twin Peaks" did this to an extent; how long the camera lingered on a ringing phone, how long a character's sobbing outbursts lasted, signaled the viewer that the storyteller was creating a world outside the norm. The amount of screen time, emphasis, and personal information revealed in Agent Cooper's undisguised relish of coffee and donuts were part of what made that story, and the storytelling in it, so unique. As audience members, right away you could tell you were into new territory. "What else did this storyteller have to tell you that you hadn't heard or seen before?"

That's because the audience instinctively expects a ratio of duration and time to story importance. As a result, too fast usually seems comedic, as in jerky, fast-paced silent comedies or zany comedy skits in which important events are compressed within time, while prolonging the screen time too much seems melodramatic, as in daytime soaps, which are infamous for dragging out story lines. In the first example, the audience doesn't have enough time to adjust and so things seem absurdly rushed, while in the second example, the audience has too much time to develop expectations of the payoff, and so no matter what finally happens it always seems anticlimactic and predictable.

5. Scale

Some examples of movies that use big *scale* are *Superman, Hunt for Red October*, and *Jurassic Park*; the vistas are sweeping, the issues affect the entire world, and the impending change is on a grand scale.

In contrast, films on a smaller scale would be the more intimate stories of *The Accidental Tourist* or *Come Back to the Five-and-Dime, Jimmy Dean, Jimmy Dean*. Those are personal stories set in confined spaces about small moments of change, although that is not to say that the change is unimportant.

6. Proportion

Understanding and using proportion in your story can also convey powerful story dynamics.

In terms of narrative style, *Avalon* was a very moving example of this sense of small moments changing lives, in contrast to a more expansive portrait of many family members over a period of years. *Dances with Wolves* also used such a contrast brilliantly, setting the private moments when Kevin Costner was alone in the fort against the sweeping epic shots of the buffalo hunts, for example.

It can also be effective to twist the audience's expectations. *Honey, I've Shrunk the Kids* had a field day with that concept in terms of physical objects; the original *Unfaithfully Yours*, by comedy genius Preston Sturges, flipped our expectations of easy and hard, in a film about a jealous husband who plots the perfect murder of his wife.

7. Physical Proximity

The *physical distance* between the viewers and the objects can also be used to orchestrate their emotional impact. In general the further away from the norm things are, the more impact it will have on viewers.

For example, in *A Clockwork Orange*, there is a closeup of an eyelid being pried open, which gives added visceral impact to the moment. In contrast, the distance between the viewers and the photographed lovers in *Blow Up* adds mystery and suspense; a similar dynamic is used with sound in *The Conversation*.

8. Emotional Proximity

The same dynamic occurs with the *emotional proximity* in a film. Loosely equivalent to a novelist's choice of first, second, or third person, emotional proximity determines how much intimacy you allow viewers to have about the real thoughts and feelings of the characters. This is a very powerful way to create bonding with characters, and a powerful area of style, which gives a story resonance, yet is one of the most rarely considered.

The Last Emperor is a brilliant use of emotional proximity in the "faraway" mode. Not only were there epic visuals, long shots, and great vistas, but even the most personal moments of the main character's life were impersonally conveyed with rigid formality. All of this combined to restate the driving dynamic of the film, which was that the emperor was a human being who was never allowed normal emotional intimacy because of his position. Everyone in the film had reasons for treating him like a pawn of history rather than a human being, and despite the strong sense of sympathy and compassion viewers developed for the character, they were never allowed to have real empathy or emotional recognition that could be expressed as "I've felt like that a million times."

Instead, viewers were forced to desire closeness through sympathy and pity, like wanting to pet an animal through a glass pane. This emotional dynamic was very potent and gave the film much of its poignancy.

An example of closer emotional proximity is a film like *Klute*, in which the audience sees Jane Fonda's character in medium closeup talking to her psychiatrist, while hearing her uncensored description of her inner drives. This allows the audience to have intimate knowledge of her emotional state, her motivations, desires, and fears, enabling them to bond with her through a sense of identification with her motives, despite the distance from her way of life.

An example of even closer authorial distance is seen in *A Christmas Story*, in which the entire story is seen through the character's eyes. Set in the thirties, this film is a delightful example of emotional proximity in which the lead character, a young boy, agonizes through the ordeals of growing up. The audience actually *sees* and hears his thoughts and fantasies. "The Wonder Years" employed a similar dynamic on television.

Where on the spectrum of emotional proximity your script falls has a lot to do with what kind of hero you're writing about. Idol heroes often benefit from a degree of emotional distance, while Everyman, underdog, and lost soul heroes are often enriched by closer emotional proximity.

9. Narrative Style

Narrative style has a lot to do with the dynamic created by comparing and contrasting the words and visual images of our story. In some films the two are very much in synch, while in others obvious contrast (if not contradiction) creates an entirely new dimension in storytelling.

Raising Arizona is a wonderful example of the contrast between words and narrative. For example, the lead character describes a beautiful sunset while viewers see the tawdriest, shabby domestic scene, yet it is exactly this romantic view of such a shabby world that endears the character to viewers. *All That Jazz* employs the same technique to create a more cynical tone, using the contrast between the choreographer's self-mocking commentary and images of physical exhaustion to convey the depth of his self-destructiveness.

It isn't necessary to have a narrator in order to use this technique. Any characters who look at their experiences from a different perspective can create wonderful territory that can be richly explored through inventive use of style.

10. Flow

Another arena of style choices has to do with the narrative *flow* of your story. Many scripts employ an invisible connection between scenes, which means that the script attempts to move through the sequence of scenes without any conspicuous gaps, while a more consciously choppy flow can create strong curiosity or suspense for viewers.

Both the book and the film of *The World According to Garp* used this stylistic device by making viewers wait a conspicuously long time to find out about the death of Robin Williams' child after a car accident.

Another example is *Charade*, which employed a series of constant surprises.

You should make a conscious choice about which kind of narrative flow would be most beneficial for your script: whether to give or withhold knowledge, how to divide knowledge between audience and characters, when to emphasize or deemphasize, and whether to tell the truth or not.

Tone: The Sum of the Parts

The total statement made by the sum of your style choices will ultimately combine to create a script's *tone*.

Consider the difference between *Dangerous Liaisons* and *Valmont*. Both of these films presented the same story; however, their tone differs completely. *Dangerous Liaisons* is a portrait of a brittle, dangerous world; sharp, hard, dramatic—it can be seen in the characters, their behavior, their motivation, the language, the costumes. In contrast, *Valmont* was on a much more human scale; the characters and goals were more accessible, and this was reflected in the softer colors, less starched costumes, and more identifiable motives.

How To Determine Your Style

Your dramatic center is the compass that you use to create and combine individual style elements without losing sight of their harmony and function within the whole. If you understand the core dynamics of your idea, your visceral sensation gives you great clarity on the logical and emotional aspects of your plot, character and momentum devices, telling you what stylistic choices will enhance your script.

But to express that visceral sensation most consistently demands translating it into conscious choices. This allows you to have *unity of presentation* throughout all the layers of your story, which is created by complementary style choices on all levels and layers of the script.

Here are some of the dynamics of your story that can be strengthened with an imaginative use of style, thus making the dramatic equation of your story a visceral experience, and not just an intellectualized theme or idea:

Style: Greasing the Tracks

1. Intensify the dramatic equation
2. Intensify bonding with hero
3. Establish the hero's world
4. Intensify the antagonists
5. Establish the "world" (defined by the antagonist's values)
6. Emphasize the matchup of hero and obstacle course
7. Contrast the hero and the world
8. Separate the hero and the world
9. Convey unity
10. Create a "signature"

QUESTIONS

Here are some questions to help you make sure that you are using style to enhance the core of your story:

1. What is the dramatic center of your story? the dramatic equation?
   What style choices will intensify them?
2. What kind of qualities do the emotions/sensations have?
   Prolonged and slow, like suspense?
   Sudden, shocking, jagged, like surprise?
   Lilting, pastoral, like happiness?
3. What kind of contrasts of emotional states would best create your desired roller coaster?
4. What would best convey the essence of the hero's world and his world view?
5. What kind of bond between viewers and characters do you want to build?
6. Where on the style spectrum is your story most effective?
7. What are the significant revealing details that convey key information in your story?
8. Consider whether you are using at all and/or using well the following:
   Scale: big or small?
   Proportion: norm or flipped?
   Proximity: close or far (physically and emotionally)?
   Authorial distance: first, second, third person?
   Color: Is it consistent with other elements?
   Texture: What adjective describes your script?
   Rhythm: fast, slow, or varied?
   Duration: Would changes in duration enhance your idea?
   Flow: smooth or choppy?
9. Is your style streamlined, transparent, theatrical?
10. How are you using style to enhance your dramatic equation?

TWELVE

Creating the
Individual Scene

Once you understand the major components of story roller coasters, it's time to construct your own. You must create somewhere between 40 and 70 individual scenes that hold the audience's moment-to-moment interest while they also fulfill their function within your overall roller-coaster design. Just as each cell in your body contains the entire DNA code, each scene in your screenplay should contribute to the dynamics of the dramatic equation, which leads viewers to experience the dramatic center of your story.

Because you must always keep these dual functions in mind, writing a truly compelling screenplay is similar in many ways to being an architect. It is absolutely crucial that an architect understand all of the structural necessities to build a house, but no buyers walk in and decide they like it because they tap their feet on the floor and ask, "So, how much pressured steel is in this beam?" Rather, they look at the beauty of the view, the size of the doorways, and the detail in the woodwork—the experiential details that are on the surface, yet cannot exist without a firm foundation underneath. To be a successful architect, you must deal with both aspects of your discipline: the structural logic needed to create the home and the buyer's subjective reaction.

The same is true for screenwriters. Knowing how to build a story roller coaster and knowing why you have created your roller coaster as you did is equivalent to the architect's technical knowledge. That analytical view of your roller coaster is *author logic*. However, the sensations that determine whether an audience finds the roller-coaster material emotionally satisfying are similar to the buyer's aesthetic concerns, and that subjective reaction is the *audience experience*. Although audience experience is ultimately dependent on the decisions made through author logic, its concerns are very different. A successful writer will deal with both.

We have already talked about how to determine what "big picture" story information to include in your scenes. Once you know what you want to convey in your scene, you have two tools with which to convey the information—stage directions and dialogue.

Constructing a Scene

Here are some thoughts to keep in mind as you create your scenes:

1. Every scene must have a clearly defined story pillar.

Each scene in your completed script should have a clear purpose, both in terms of advancing the audience's understanding of the story and in contributing to the overall construction of the roller-coaster design. The "audience experience" function of a scene is to convey the story information necessary to track the logical and emotional progression of change. For example, one scene may convey the fact that a couple has broken up, while the next might convey the husband's sadness. However, scenes also have a structural purpose as well. The "author logic" or structural function is creating the right-height story pillar for that section of the roller coaster. To further the above example, the scene in which the couple splits up could provide a big spike of surprise, while the following scene of quiet regret provides a momentary lull. That's why it's so helpful to have a sense of the script's structure.

In order to address the audience experience aspect of your scene, you must be very clear about the key changes in your story, the plot and character arcs, the central idea of what the characters' motives and goals are, what is at stake in this scene, who wins and who loses, and what the characters' attitudes are toward the result. To service the author logic, you must make sure that you know how high the story pillar is supposed to be, and how you intend to achieve that height.

2. No story pillar can be neutral.

Because of the audience's hunger for new information and emotional attachment, a scene's impact can't be neutral. The audience always experiences the next pillar as higher or lower than the previous one. Therefore, you should avoid including scenes that only set up future events, because if the audience can't find a clear story pillar within the scene, they will feel a sense of disappointment, causing their experience of the roller coaster to sag.

The audience wants reassurances that the effort will be worthwhile, that the message conveyed in the dramatic equation is valid, that the author knows the world of the story, and that the effort to become equally familiar will prove worthwhile.

You need to establish authority, credibility, and trustworthiness. An audience can sense a storyteller not in command as a horse can sense a rider's apprehension. They will sense whether they can trust the storyteller, if they are being taken somewhere new and different, and if the story has something worthwhile to say. The moment the author gives inaccurate, useless, or inconsistent information, the audience begins to withdraw, stopping whatever momentum there was.

3. Every story pillar should contribute to the dramatic equation.

If you were doing a quick outline of your script and were told to boil each scene down to one sentence, that sentence would probably be the story pillar of the scene, the key piece of information to which you are consciously drawing the audience's attention. Although they may not be aware of it, viewers are looking for that story pillar, that click of the scene as they put together the mosaic of your story, and if they do not discover it, they will lack a sense of completion by the end of the scene.

Another danger emerges as the viewers look for the scene click: if they don't find it, they may assign that significance to some other aspect of the scene and thereby accidentally twist the focus or meaning of your story.

The way to guard against such misunderstandings is to make sure every scene in your script has a clear purpose, both within the audience's experience and the author logic. The "headline" is the obvious, face-value purpose of the scene in terms of audience experience, while the "small print" is the author logic, structural function, which may or may not even be apparent to the viewers. However, even if it is, then it should seem secondary to the headline function, which is the audience's conscious understanding of the story pillar at the time.

4. Every scene should address the four audience needs.

Each scene must also fulfill at least one of the four audience needs of *new information, bonding, conflict resolution*, and *completion*. In fact, as a general rule, the more you can address each one in a scene, the more intrigued the audience will be. However, when trying to address more than one need, make sure they work in coordination, rather than competing for the audience's attention. One good way to do that is to decide which one should function as the headline of the scene while the others serve as small print.

5. Come in late and leave early.

Screen time is valuable, and the audience's hunger for new information is strong. Therefore you should only include the information the audience will perceive as directly related to your story pillar. Viewers quickly become impatient when a scene is padded. The more you can trim your scene down to just the core information, the richer the story will seem and the stronger the momentum. Audiences quickly realize that they have to stay on their toes with a story that moves briskly, and briskness alone will create a sense of eagerness and curiosity.

6. Avoid clutter.

For the same reason, avoid clutter. Filling screen time with trivia undercuts the scene's impact, so unless it is somehow important to your overall roller coaster, keep it to a minimum. For example, a scene in which a group of people are introducing themselves probably does not contain enough new information to be worth screen time unless, for example, one of the characters uses a name the audience knows is fake, or someone is abnormally shy. That kind of information could be valuable for arousing curiosity and/or advancing the story line, but usually it is tedious and should be cut.

Writers have trouble streamlining their scenes, and their reasoning is "that's what would happen in real life." But forget real life—the screen is not real life. Instead, it is a distillation of life, and you should present distilled information. Occurrences in real life can last any amount of time; your screenplay can only last approximately 120 minutes. You must evaluate every word in your scenes with that limitation in mind.

The audience is looking for direction and will often take things literally, so avoid filling your opening scenes with decorative clutter and instead provide information that deals directly with the story.

7. Keep exposition to a minimum.

In many ways, exposition is like that initial time spent on a roller coaster when the cars are pulled uphill until they are high enough to let the fun part of the ride begin. It's not the most fun part of the ride, but it's necessary.

In a story roller coaster, you want to keep the exposition to an absolute minimum, especially at the outset when the audience already feels an innate sense of resistance, as we've already discussed.

8. Transitions between scenes are important.

You should give careful thought to how your scenes progress in transition from one to the next. It may involve the last line of dialogue in one scene and the first line in the next, or an action scene flowing into an exposition scene, or one action scene bumping into another one.

Juxtapose your scenes in a logically evocative way. Notice how they "feel" next to each other. Each scene needs to lead to the next, tracking some aspect of change within the story. The connection can be straightforward cause and effect or something more subtle than that. But scenes that come later in the script must answer the questions in the audience's mind. The scene flow should also illuminate your story arc, connecting scenes in a way that makes the changes in the story seem natural or at least credible. The sequence of plot events conveys the rational logic of your story, while the pattern of emotional change that a lead character undergoes is the emotional arc of your story.

You can also create sequences linked by rhythm and pacing, as in the garage dance sequence in *Foot Loose*; by location, as in *Around the World in Eighty Days*; by time, in period and contemporary sequences, as in *The French Lieutenant's Woman*; or by intent, as in the training sequences in *Rocky*.

Stage Directions

The first major tool to convey information to readers are *stage directions*, which are responsible for conveying the visual information in your scene. There are some key things you need to remember about stage directions:

1. Keep stage directions short.

By saying you should *keep your stage directions short*, I don't mean that you shouldn't have a very clear sense of what the scenes look like, how the characters behave, and what kind of setting there is. You must see every scene vividly in your mind; the writer who can't see or hear the scene taking place is going to have difficulty making it come alive for readers. However, there is a big difference between seeing each detail in your mind and forcing the reader to envision the scene exactly as you would like to see it filmed.

Remember that the stage directions for a script are only the "instruction manual" to make a movie. Their only function is to create the kinds of sensations and feelings in readers that make them feel as though they are seeing the completed movie in their minds. Their function is *not* to describe every thought that goes through your mind while imagining a scene; that's not necessary to understanding your story, nor is it the best way to share it.

This writing flaw is most often caused by writers' attempts to describe the scene precisely as envisioned in their minds. It's as though they believe the only way to capture the power of the moment is to describe every element of the scene in minute detail. Ironically, weighing your script down with unnecessary detail will work against your desire to make the reader feel the vitality of the moment.

There are many reasons why you should learn to restrain yourself. One is that conveying the precise images in your head into someone else's head is impossible. You can convey the tone, the mood, a general sense of location, for instance, but *exactly* what the table looks like is too detailed and still guarantees nothing about the reader's reaction to your tale. Think about your own experience: a friend describes someone to you, complete with gestures and vocal expressions; you think you have an accurate mental picture, but then you meet the person and realize that your image was completely wrong.

Another reason for restraining yourself is more practical than creative. Most people in this business have so much reading to do in their work that thick, long paragraphs in a script cause their enthusiasm to drop dramatically. They assume as a result of long, painful experience that thick prose means the writer has been unable to organize the information according to its importance, and that they are about to plunge into long passages where only a few pieces of information are vital. The emotional power of the scene can be lost as the result of overwritten stage directions, and in the process, author credibility suffers. The reader begins to wonder, "If the writer doesn't know what's really important, how likely is it that this story will ultimately pay off?"

2. Focus on relaying the essence of the scene.

Rather than describing every image that comes to mind when you think of a scene, try selecting one or two *revealing details* that convey the rest. For example, if you are writing a scene about a woman who is pretending to be rich, you don't need to describe every item of clothing she's wearing. You'll be more effective by simply mentioning that the sleeves of her silk blouse are frayed or that the price tag from the thrift shop can be seen on her collar.

Leave room for the reader's imagination to intermingle with your revealing details; the interaction encourages readers to personalize their involvement. Just as radio was the "theater of the mind," allowing the audience to grab hold of a scene and fill in images that were most relevant to their experience, short pertinent stage directions let your readers imagine their own most vivid image of "a greasy spoon" or "a millionaire's mansion."

3. Use visually evocative words.

Another way to convey the essence of a scene quickly is through imaginative *word choice*. There's a huge difference in the visual images created by the phrases "A boat passes by" and "A white yacht glides past."

Similarly, where you choose to set your scene, as well as how you describe that setting, can add texture and tension. For example, a love scene in a library will feel very different from the same dialogue spoken on the beach.

4. Use emotionally evocative words.

Using verbs that convey attitude and atmosphere can also add impact to your script. However, try to focus your efforts on strong descriptions of visual information, rather than on adding lots of "running commentary." The latter can often seem too smart-alecky and distracting. There's another problem, too, if the characters and dialogue aren't as interesting as the commentary (which happens fairly often); the characters will seem even blander by contrast.

5. Create a sense of action.

It is important that the essential energy of your story be conveyed in the visual images of your screenplay rather than just in the dialogue. It's important to convey the major actions and reactions that the characters have, but long, detailed descriptions will actually work against the sense of speed and excitement needed to make those scenes work best.

As a result, some writers limit themselves to two-line descriptions in each paragraph, even if there must be ten such paragraphs to describe the scene. This concise style is particularly important for action scenes, which need to seem fast and exciting.

6. Write stage directions in the present tense.

Writing stage directions in the present tense creates greater immediacy and impact. The past tense separates readers from the moment and distances them from the story.

7. Don't include camera angles.

Choosing the camera angle is the director's job. If you insist on making those choices, you don't allow the director's imagination to grab hold of the script and see it through his or her own eyes. Additionally, the images that are so exciting for you because of the information in your negative space may actually work against the director's sense of excitement or may be less compelling than those which could be imagined if your stage directions weren't hampering his ability to come to the script without preconceptions.

The only time to include a camera angle is when it is essential to understanding a scene. Making it clear to readers that the audience will see a man's legs during the murder sequence but never his face may be enough reason, but even then it's better to describe what the scene would look like rather than what camera angle should be used to achieve that look.

The second major tool you have with which to convey information in your screenplay is *dialogue*, the language that the audience will hear on the screen.

On the stage, the fact that there are physical constraints of time and place demand that dialogue carry a great deal of the dramatic "weight." But the screen is predominantly a visual medium, so words rarely have the same impact as they do on the stage. As a result, conventional wisdom claims that dialogue is not of primary importance in a screenplay; in fact, Hitchcock has been credited with saying, "Build your screenplay first, then add dialogue." That may be a bit extreme, but the point is that the real power of a screenplay comes from the dramatic equation and the overall roller-coaster ride, not the conversation.

Because it creates a "first impression" of your screenplay, dialogue is of great importance. The way a writer uses dialogue is very revealing. Good dialogue shows that a writer understands people and has an ear for how they talk. Bad dialogue instantly impairs author credibility. The moment professionals read a script with stilted, talky, or overly theatrical dialogue, they begin to suspect the writer does not have the skill to create a compelling script. As soon as those doubts set in, the writer is working uphill to prove himself.

Here are some tips for writing credible dialogue:

1. Know what your characters want to say.

If you are struggling with dialogue in your screenplay, it may be because you aren't really sure what your characters want or need to say. Once you can get clear on the characters' intentions and desires, you may find that the words come easily. If not, try asking yourself, "What's the point of this line?" Putting the character's thoughts into your own words, and then translating that idea into the character's unique manner of expression may help give you clarity.

2. Characters should have distinctive voices.

Most writers have a "voice" that permeates their entire script (including stage directions) unless they make a conscious and determined effort to differentiate. As a result, all their characters tend to talk with the same rhythm, pacing, humor, sensibility, and vocabulary.

Creating a *distinctive voice* for each character is important and can be a powerful way to make them come alive. Think about Al Pacino's character in *Scent of a Woman*, or Archie Bunker in "All in the Family."

A character's voice is conveyed through word choice, phrasing, mannerisms, attitudes, and tone. One way to practice writing distinctive dialogue is to imagine a specific person conveying the information you want your character to say. For example, how would your best friend give street directions? How would your favorite teacher? Notice different word choices, points of reference, mannerisms, slang. Focus on personal speech styles and try to include and convey those distinctions in your dialogue. Also try comparing each of your characters to the other. How would your hero say a line? How would the antagonist convey the same information? How would your mother?

3. Keep character voices consistent.

Often characters' voices are clear and distinct at the beginning of the screenplay, when the writer's concentration is on establishing the characters. However, as soon as the plot begins, the characters lose their distinctiveness and become stick figures, expressing themselves in a very generic way. So make a special effort to create and maintain your characters' voices throughout, because that will significantly strengthen the script's credibility.

4. Dialogue should be consistent with the story's style.

Similar to the choices available to you in the overall style of your script, you can choose to make your dialogue "transparent," "theatrical," or "streamlined."

Transparent dialogue sounds like everyday speech and is usually the best choice unless there is a conspicuously important aspect you want to emphasize. Transparent dialogue keeps the focus on the information being conveyed rather than on the "packaging," as anything other than realistic dialogue tends to call attention to itself. Keep the dialogue on screen focused on new information. Cluttering the movie with social chatter, unless you have an important point to make, is not a good use of screen time.

Theatrical dialogue calls attention to itself, whether it's the street-smart period dialogue of a Sam Spade detective film, the wild chatter of Peter O'Toole in *The Conformist*, nearly all the characters in *A Clockwork Orange*, or any other stylized use of words. The further away something is from the norm, the more attention it draws, so you want to use such a theatrical element with precision and clarity.

Streamlined dialogue is minimal, unnaturally terse, even staccato. An example of streamlined dialogue might be Arnold Schwarzenegger's dialogue in *Terminator 2*, which was conspicuously abrupt. Many action characters tend to speak in such a manner. The style of speech emphasizes and intentionally reinforces the difference between the character and ordinary people.

5. Dialogue should convey attitude.

Dialogue that adequately conveys information but no attitude seems lifeless and artificial. That's because in real life, people have attitudes about everything. Even a quick question like "What time is it?" can convey attitude— such as "I must be really late" or "Isn't this lecture over yet?"

Dialogue can also convey characters' attitude toward themselves. Characters express themselves very differently depending on how comfortable they are saying what's being said. For example, the words and phrasing a shy woman would use to invite someone to dinner are quite different from the same invitation extended by a bold, confident woman.

6. Action speaks louder than words.

If you've ever tried to express yourself during an argument or when your heart is filled with despair, you know how difficult it is even to put your feelings into words, let alone well-chosen ones. To expect characters to do that makes them seem contrived.

The reason for this type of impact is that, in general, dialogue is better at expressing thoughts than emotions. If you intend to convey an emotion, consider whether there's an action or gesture that would express the feeling more effectively than language. Also think about whether something should be included in stage directions rather than in dialogue, or if it really needs to be conveyed to the audience at all.

Some writers are convinced that readers cannot understand the character or story unless they are told every thought, but, as with stage directions, usually that much detail detracts from rather than enriches a script.

7. Avoid long speeches.

Although a few big speeches can work on stage, long speeches on screen tend to make viewers feel restless. Because film is a visual medium, audiences take in information far more easily with their eyes than with their ears.

8. Dialogue must have a realistic flow.

There's nothing more awkward than a character asking a question followed by a long declarative sentence, and then having the other character respond to the question. That's not how people really talk so it seems stilted and artificial.

9. Listen to the dialogue you write.

Avoid two-fers. These are what I call lines of dialogue that combine two dissimilar thoughts into one speech. "Go to hell, Jake. (pause) By the way, did you stop at the store?" is an example of a two-fer. This manner of speaking should be avoided unless you are using it deliberately to establish a character's distracted or confused state of mind. Two-fers convey the impression that the author doesn't know how to write dialogue, causing an immediate decline in author credibility.

To avoid constructing two-fers, separate them, if only with a quick one-word response from the other character.

QUESTIONS

Here are some questions to help ensure that you are creating vivid and effective scenes:

1. SCENES

1. What is the story pillar of your scene?
   Is it a load-bearing one?
   What is the headline, author logic function?
   What is the small print, audience experience function?
   What is the scene click?

2. Where is this pillar in the overall design of your roller coaster? Up? Down? Why?
   What speed?
   Is it a key moment?
   Does it change the direction, speed, etc.?
   How?

3. What is at stake in this scene?

4. What is each character's goal in the scene?
   What is the attitude?
   Does it advance the heroes' internal motivation? External plans?
   Who wants what?
   Who gets what they want and why?
   Who doesn't, and why?
   What is their reaction to the win or loss?

5. How does your scene address the need for
   New information?
   Bonding?
   Conflict resolution?
   Completion?

6. How does it advance your plot?
   Characterizations?
   Momentum?

7. How is momentum established or created?

8. Is anything set up?
   Is anything paid off?
   As foreshadowing?
   As a planted seed? If it's a planted seed, how is it disguised?

9. What questions does the scene answer?
   What new questions does it plant in viewers' minds?
   What are the central *how* or *why* questions?
   Is it a *how* or *why* story?
10. Does the setting heighten the emotional impact?
   Style?
   Dialogue?
   Stage directions?
11. How does this scene connect to your dramatic equation and your dramatic center?

2. STAGE DIRECTIONS

12. Are they as short as you can possibly make them?
13. What is the essence of each scene?
   What are the revealing details?
14. What are you doing to make them visually powerful?
   Emotionally intense?
15. How is information visually conveyed?

3. DIALOGUE

16. What are your characters trying to say?
   What are they comfortable saying?
17. Are your character voices distinctive?
18. What is being conspicuously unsaid?
   Does it need to be said?
   Would it be more powerful as an action?
   Is it more powerful in silence?
19. What dialogue style is best for your script?
   Transparent?
   Streamlined?
   Theatrical?
20. Are speeches too long?

THIRTEEN

Testing Your Roller Coaster

Now you've built your roller coaster, element by element. But before you open it to the public at large, you need to do some test runs to make sure that it creates the sensations it was designed to deliver. There are two things you want to check. One is whether the highs and lows, curves and twists, textures and speeds all function as you intend, while the other is to make sure that the roller-coaster ride, even if it functions as designed, provides an enveloping experience for your riders.

The intended design of your roller coaster, as well as the resulting choices you made to construct it, are a reflection of your *author's logic*. For example, your roller coaster may have been intended to have the design shown at the top of page 164.

Testing Your Roller Coaster

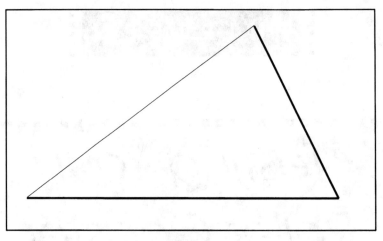

Author Logic

However, the actual sensations that people have when riding your roller coaster are the *audience experience*, and the roller coaster they actually experience may look like this:

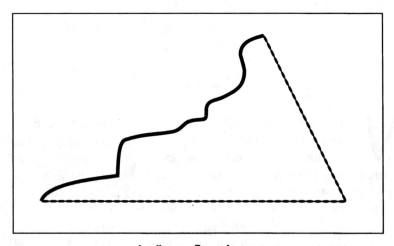

Audience Experience

Ideally the tracks of those two roller coasters should be the same, but often that is not the case, especially in first drafts. In fact, it is normal to have at least small discrepancies, and sometimes there are major differences. Those gaps between the roller coaster you intended and the ride the audience actually takes are the "Bermuda Triangles" of stories.

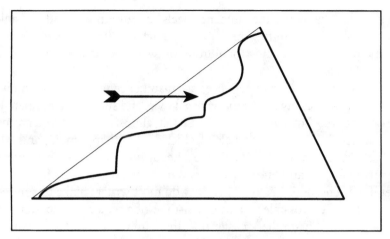

The "Bermuda Triangle" of Stories

Your goal is to create a screenplay where author logic and audience experience are the same. Therefore, after you complete a draft of your screenplay, you must evaluate whether there is a difference between author logic and audience experience, and if so, where and why. Then you can proceed to make whatever changes are necessary.

The main reason there can be such "black holes" is not because it's impossible to synch up these two lines, but because most writers don't even recognize that the difference between author logic and audience experience may exist. You must always be aware that the essence of the story experience takes place in the viewers' heads, not on the page or on the screen. No matter how eloquent a case you make for why an audience *should* feel a certain way, "the customer is always right." It is your responsibility to make sure that you have consciously addressed this challenge and used your craftsmanship to ensure the ride that you, the artist, intended to create.

When a Roller Coaster Doesn't Work

The reason Bermuda Triangle gaps exist between the writer's intention and the audience experience is that the writer guessed incorrectly about the height of the story pillars. The writer has overestimated the intensity of the audience's reaction to a piece of story information, and viewers sense that they are supposed to be having a more powerful reaction than they are actually having.

When that happens, the audience feels an unsettling kind of sinking sensation, almost like hitting an "air pocket," which disrupts their concentration, momentarily distancing them from the story and hampering the overall emotional build.

Think about your own experiences as an audience member. You know the sensation. You're sitting there, enjoying a movie, and suddenly a moment feels false or contrived. You feel a small internal jolt, almost as though you are losing your balance for a second. You also feel let down, disappointed, and a little wary about whether the ride is going to falter again. It's a distinctly unpleasant feeling for viewers, and one that writers want to avoid at all cost.

Yet if the sensation is so obvious, why do most writers make this mistake? Because it's never possible to take a first-time ride on a roller coaster you've built, and it's that first roller-coaster ride, the "virgin reaction," that evokes the clearest sensations.

Virgin Reaction

When someone initially reads a script or sees a movie, they have a *virgin reaction* because they have no knowledge—and therefore no expectations—of upcoming story events. During that virgin ride, the viewers' logic and emotions experience the story exactly as it is, with their gut reactions indicating clearly what is not working.

Among the sensations the audience may feel during a virgin reaction are the click of recognition when they realize the importance of a load-bearing pillar, the "tightening of the screw" sensation when a story pillar adds to the mounting dramatic tension, or the "ugh!" when a story pillar conspicuously fails to reach its potential height.

If you have read someone else's script, you know how easy it is to see what's working and what's not. However, read that script a second time, and you will see how different your reactions are. Some things that were confusing the first time won't bother you the second and vice versa. That's because you have a sense of where the story is going, and your mind begins to fill in the blanks.

Virgin reactions are extremely valuable because they enable the writer to be most in touch with what an audience feels. Yet losing touch with the virgin reaction is an unavoidable part of the creative process, because writers who know their own script well enough to anticipate events can never experience their own story from the audience's point of view. It's what is meant by a writer being "too close" to the work.

So there's the essence of your dilemma: If you can never get on and take the ride for yourself, how can you tell if your roller coaster provides the ride you intended? How do you overcome the built-in subjectivity you have as the writer? The answer is you have to get accurate feedback from someone riding your roller coaster for the first time.

Letting Others Take a "Test Ride"

In order to make the most of the secondhand information you will get when you ask someone to read your script, you need to have a clear idea of what you want your audience/reader to feel as they go through your story. Then you must assess how well your intended roller-coaster design matches what your readers experience.

Here are some guidelines for making sure that you get the most accurate feedback possible:

1. Know what you want your audience to feel.

The entire basis for your roller-coaster design is knowing precisely how you want your audience to feel, not just by the end of your screenplay, but at every stage along the way. What emotions do you want your audience to experience, in what order, and to what intensity? Be prepared to articulate these answers.

If you've done your homework, you should have a very clear notion of what you want the audience to be thinking and feeling at any given moment in your story, what questions you want them to have, what assumptions you want them to make, whose side you want them to take in arguments, what expectations you want them to form by what point in the story. As though you could graph your story, you should know exactly where the highs and lows should be and what causes them. That is the pattern that creates the story roller coaster for the audience, so you should know exactly what responses would create the ideal ride. If, as you listen to the feedback, you hear answers that are different from the ones you expected, you will be able to locate the exact placement of your Bermuda Triangle.

2. Choose your audience carefully.

In order to trust the feedback you get, you must really trust the person, in terms of overall aesthetic taste, ability to articulate reactions, and credibility.

Pick someone who you think will tell you their true reactions, not just what they think you may want to hear. It's also a good idea to pick someone who likes the same kind of movies you do. By doing this, you are not trying to "stack the deck" by asking people whose responses are usually in keeping with yours, but someone whose sensibilities you trust.

3. Know what audience you are writing for.

Know who and what your intended audience is, and be honest with yourself: Is the reader you've selected a good sampling of that audience? If your story is geared toward young teens, is your grandmother really the best person to go on the test ride? If you decide to show it to her anyway, should you panic if she thinks it's too "silly"?

4. Word your questions neutrally.

It's tempting to ask your readers, "Did you like my script?", but most of the time, it doesn't yield useful information. One reason is that most people won't want to hurt your feelings, and such loaded language makes it hard for them to be completely honest about any weaknesses. Even if they do like it, such vague questions really only ask the reader, "How does it compare to your idea of what the story should be?"

So be specific, but try not to use judgmental words. Ask questions that people aren't hesitant to answer. For example, don't ask, "Were you bored?" Rather ask, "What did you expect to happen on page 100?" That kind of neutral question allows them to respond with specific observations rather than judgments and will make the feedback much more valuable.

What you need to know as clearly as possible is what the roller-coaster ride felt like to them—where they went up, where they went down, where it felt slow or fast, where they found the sensations satisfying and where they did not. You need to know what they were feeling and when in order to track whether your roller coaster is creating the structure that you want the riders to perceive.

5. Translate the answers.

George Bernard Shaw once wrote, "Most people can tell you there's a problem, but it takes a genius to tell you how to fix it." People can usually tell when there's something wrong with a script, and they can even spot the moment where the problem becomes obvious. But trying to determine exactly what's causing the problem and what needs to be changed can be a lot more difficult.

So ask for and listen to your readers' reactions, but don't take their comments or suggestions too literally. Instead, like a doctor examining a patient, focus your energy on hearing the symptoms described rather than accepting their self-diagnosis at face value.

Even professionals can find it difficult to express their instinctive reactions to screenplays, so you can imagine how hard it may be for a layman to express thoughts accurately. Consequently, you have to act as a translator.

For example, if a reader says, "I don't think this character is working very well" or "I don't believe the character would do that," don't let your pride get you too focused on semantics. Rather, hear the important information; something about that characterization isn't working for this reader.

Focus on understanding the essence of readers' comments. You can then attempt to get more specific by using your dramatic equation to pin down the problem.

The way this technique works is that you suggest a scenario in which all your story elements remain the same except the one in question. Ask the reader how changing that one in a certain way would affect his or her reaction. For example, you could say, "If I kept the plot events the same, but made the character more likable, would that fix the problem?" or "What if I kept the same characterization but changed the plot?" The resulting discussions can help you pinpoint the real issue.

6. Listen selectively.

Notes that help you build the roller coaster you intend to create are very useful. So are notes that confirm problem areas that have been bugging you. It's especially important to pay attention if you get the same note saying the same thing from more than one person. Even if the feedback contradicts your author logic, you need to remember that audience experience, as with beauty, is in the eye of the beholder.

7. Listen critically.

However, it's also important to remember that you can "never please all of the people all of the time." If the notes you get are telling you to build a different roller coaster from the one you intended, you should ponder extensively before you change your overall roller-coaster design.

The reason people may be giving you notes that would result in a different

Testing Your Roller Coaster

roller coaster is that they may be responding to their own dramatic center within the topic. As we've discussed before, people can have very different and unique dramatic centers because of the experiences and world view contained in their own negative spaces; therefore, suggestions to change your roller-coaster design may be prompted by their dramatic center rather than a failure of your roller coaster. If their dramatic center is not the same as yours, their notes will always lead you to build their version of the roller coaster rather than your own.

8. Understand the difference between preference and observation.

All people have their own taste in entertainment, which is why some people dislike a movie even if it's a box office smash. They simply don't enjoy that kind of topic, or roller-coaster ride, and no matter how well built that roller coaster is, their basic reaction is the same. So it's important that you understand whether the comments you are receiving are the result of established preferences or specific observations on your individual script.

For example, if you have friends who don't enjoy children's literature and don't think they are particularly good at responding to it, don't give that type of script to them. They probably wouldn't love it no matter how well it was written. On the other hand, even if they're not crazy about that kind of material, their specific observations about where it held their attention or whether they found the characters empathetic could still be useful.

Many writers assume that anyone will like a good script, or, conversely, that it is possible to write a script that everyone in the world will like. However, that simply is not true. It's vital to remember that you can't please everyone, nor is it possible to build a roller coaster that satisfies everyone in the world. No matter how compelling a roller coaster is, some people will not enjoy the ride, because of preexisting tastes and preferences that have nothing to do with your specific script. The result is that you could write exactly the script you wanted and they might not like it, or you could have failed to build the roller coaster you intended but they liked the ride they took.

9. Ask why.

That's why it's so important to get the specifics of your readers' thinking, not just the headlines. Don't settle for "yes" or "no" answers or first impressions because those are only the tips of the iceberg in terms of how they really responded to your material. It also makes it too easy for you to misunderstand the real meaning of their feedback.

Make sure you ask "Why?"—as in "Why were you surprised?" or "Why did you think the couple would break up?" The answers can be enormously useful. Rather than simply getting a reaction, you get to the root of the reaction, which gives you much greater clarity about how they experienced your screenplay.

For example, if your discussion stays on the "Did you like it—yes or no?" level, you may interpret a response like "I didn't believe the character would do that" as a major disagreement with your story, thus assuming a huge Bermuda Triangle. However, if you can get your readers to be more specific and articulate, you might discover the only reason they didn't believe it was the way the dialogue was written, or because of an assumption they developed about the character which you had not intended. That kind of revelation helps you realize that the gap isn't nearly as great as you first feared.

The discussion may reveal a different kind of insight as well. Your readers may say they didn't like a scene, which might sound as though the roller coaster didn't deliver the ride you intended at that moment, when the truth is that they may have experienced exactly what you wanted them to feel—they just didn't happen to like that sensation. Needless to say, that's a crucial distinction, so always do your best to get as much detail about your readers' reactions as possible.

10. Ask where.

It's more important to know where your readers felt various sensations and emotional reactions than to know what their final, cumulative opinion is. Therefore, you can either literally stop your readers at intervals and ask questions like, "On page 10, what did you think was going to happen?" "What did you think on page 20?" Or you can ask them those kinds of questions after they've read your whole script.

The first option tends to give you a more accurate picture of their reactions, but one way or the other, you must make sure that you understand exactly where they felt their various reactions.

11. Keep looking for your ideal reader.

My friend Oliver Hailey thought it was crucial to find that one person, that one springboard, whose reaction you could really trust, and then, as he would say, "Listen, listen, listen."

Finding that ideal reader, that person whom you trust as a sounding board, sometimes takes years, but it can make all the difference in the world if you are lucky enough to find the person.

Testing Your Roller Coaster

I know from experience. At first I had a hard time writing this book, because I had taught the material so many times. It was difficult for me to be sure I was expressing the ideas on paper clearly to someone who wasn't already familiar with them. Then my very good friend Jan Wildman offered to be my sounding board, and my entire sense of writing the book changed overnight!

Suddenly I didn't have to spend emotional or intellectual energy wondering if a segment was working, or which order ideas should be in. I knew Jan's taste and understanding of the material was completely fresh yet accurate, so I suddenly had a mirror whose reflection I could trust. I also had faith in her honesty and kindness. I knew that she would tell me the truth, but I also knew that she would not laugh at me (something that all writers fear!). The point is, I felt safe creatively and emotionally, and the book really took off after that.

QUESTIONS TO ASK YOURSELF

Here are sample questions that you might mull over in relation to your script. The questions you need to ask will be specific to your screenplay, but these may get you started:

1. What roller coaster did you intend to build?
2. What emotional reactions do you want readers to have?
3. Where are your intended highs and lows?
    Built on what expectations, preferences, doubts?
4. What do you want them to feel at the beginning of the story?
    In the middle?
    At each key event?
    At the pivotal moment?
    At the climax?
    At the end result?
5. Where should the audience feel surprise?
    Curiosity?
    Suspense?
6. Where should the audience feel hope?
    Dread?
    Excitement?
7. What questions should they be asking?
    Where should they find the answers?
8. When should they feel drawn to the characters, and when repelled?
9. How should they feel at the end?
    What should they want to happen?
10. What should they think is the point of the story?
    Should they agree with your dramatic equation or not?

QUESTIONS TO ASK YOUR READERS

Here are some sample questions for your reader(s). You should already know exactly what you want to hear in response.

1. What is this story about?
   Tell me the story in your own words.
2. What first got your interest? Why?
   When did you lose interest? Why?
   On page 10, what did you expect to happen?
   On page 20? 30? 40? (or whatever pages apply)
   Did you want it to happen?
   Why or why not?
3. Did this script focus on the aspect of the story you found most interesting?
   If not, where would you have liked to see it go?
   Where did you expect it to go?
   Would you have enjoyed that more?
   Why?
4. What new information did you learn from "X" scene?
   Did it tell you anything new about the world?
5. What do you feel about the characters?
   What emotions did you feel for the hero? Villain?
   Empathy? Sympathy? Disinterest? Why?
   Whose side were you on? Why?
   When did you feel connected to the characters?
   Distanced?
6. What questions were you eager to have answered on page x? Why?
7. Did you change your mind about any of the characters as the story progressed?
8. What are the key revelations in the story?
   Were you surprised by anything?
   Confused by anything?
9. What would you say was the message of the story?
   Do you agree with that message?
10. Do you think it was worth telling?
    Why?

FOURTEEN

Fixing Your Roller Coaster

Now you have a sense of where your roller coaster is working and where it's not. Chances are that some aspect of your story is not having the impact you intended, and so the final step in creating a great screenplay is the rewrite(s). Here are some techniques for making the most of this final phase of bringing your script to life.

▪ Let Your Script Cool as Long as Possible ▪

Often at this point you have so many conflicting images and impulses, you're not sure which ones to listen to. Which ones are important? Which are most consistent with what you're trying to say?

The best thing you can do when getting ready to rewrite your script is to let it get "cold," which means leaving your script alone for a while so that you can forget as much of your author logic as possible. The goal is to have as much of a virgin, or at least a quasi-virgin, reaction as possible to the material. As a result, the longer you let your script cool, the better. In fact, the ideal is to leave it alone long enough to totally forget what the next line of dialogue is or what the next scene will be, so that you come to the story with as fresh an eye as possible.

However, sometimes it takes months, if not years, for a script to get that cold, and often you simply won't have the time. The next best thing to do is consciously fill your mind with new stimuli to take your mind off the script. Take a vacation. Go to other kinds of movies (not the kind you are working on!). Read books, magazines. Start a project. Take up a hobby. Do anything that is *not* related to your story.

When it's finally time to read your script, that first rereading is a very important step in the process of doing a good rewrite, so do everything you can to get the maximum benefit from the experience. Go someplace where you won't be interrupted, make sure you have as much time as you will need, and then give your full attention to your script, because if you don't, it will be weeks, if not months, before you can have such a fresh and enlightening reading of your script again.

• Focus on the Big Picture •

The trick to making the most of this reading is getting a visceral awareness of the whole. It's much more important that you get a sense of the story's overall emotional build than to stop and make corrections. So rather than taking detailed notes or trying to do corrections as you go, just scribble quick "shorthand" signals to remind you of what snagged your attention.

You may think you'll remember what your first reactions were when you go back to fix segments, but you probably won't, especially if you're reading an entire script. However, if you write lengthy notes to yourself, you will lose your ability to really stay on the roller coaster, so just scribble quick notes in the margins, then keep moving forward.

• Collate Your Notes •

Once you have indicated your virgin reactions in the margin, you can go through the script more slowly. The point of the second reading is not just to look at the individual problems, but to look for recurring patterns or issues in order to understand the real cause of those problems, not just the symptoms.

Listen to your own instincts, as well as to the notes you've received from others, and try to find the connection between them. Usually a roller coaster fails because of problems with one of the four main audience needs: new information, bonding, conflict resolution, and completion. Which category would most of your notes and concerns fall into? How can you more successfully fulfill those needs and thus draw readers into your story more effectively?

▪ Go Back to Your Dramatic Center ▪

If you know that something's wrong with your roller coaster, but you're not sure what the cause is, the best thing to do is to go back to the core, to the dramatic center of your story. Have you explored the aspect of this story that most excited you? Have you communicated that aspect of the story to your readers, or do you have to sit there explaining to them what they need to know to make the material on the page compelling? If that's what you are doing, the problem may be that the essence of the story is still in your mind rather than on the page.

If you are too far from your dramatic center, you may mistakenly resort to "short-term solves." They are solutions that may fix an individual problem but do not contribute to the effectiveness of the overall ride. Not only can short-term solves break up the pattern of tension and release needed for the dramatic structure to work well, but they can also set up expectations the script never delivers on, because the writer never intended to make that promise.

Another problem may be that you never really found your dramatic center, and as a result, your story is lacking that central axis. Your dramatic center determines several crucial aspects of your script, so without it, you are probably communicating very mixed messages to your viewers at best.

If you have any doubts about whether you have found your story's dramatic center, here's one way to test to make sure you are on the right track. Take your dramatic center, which is the same quality that separates your hero from the world, and expand each of those opposing value systems to the extreme. Is that the story you want to write about? Does it line up with the separation of the hero and his world? If you play out that difference, is that the world you want to write about? If not, what do you need to change about your story in order to get it into alignment?

▪ Expand Out to Your Dramatic Equation ▪

Just as you use your dramatic center to create and clarify the essence of your story roller-coaster design, you can also use your dramatic equation to examine whether your execution is bringing your story to life.

One good way is to verbalize the statement of your dramatic equation, then check to make sure that each crucial step in that central arc of change is dramatized in your story. Remember, the dramatic equation is the skeletal statement of your story's essence: "This person, plus this series of events, equals this outcome." Are all of the necessary components there? Does the plot track? Does the character arc track? Are there any missing moments? Is the momentum building toward climax? Is there a pivotal moment when the balance of the equation tilts and change becomes inevitable? Is there a full, cathartic release?

You can also use the dramatic equation to test possible solutions before implementing them. For example, ask yourself such questions as "If I kept the same characterization but changed the character's plan would that make the script feel better?" or "If I kept the plotline but changed the character's attitudes and comments would that be closer to the sensation I'm trying to create?"

▪ Decide Where the Problem Is ▪

No matter what kind of problem you're having in your script, it always will become evident as a structural problem in which the audience experiences the "air-pocket" sensation caused by pillars that are not as tall or as strong as they need to be to support the roller coaster. As a result, you can locate where the problem becomes obvious by noticing where in your script the bulk of the notes are located.

There tend to be four major patterns of structural problems:

1. Slow Starts

This kind of roller coaster has a long, slow start before it finally begins to build effectively.

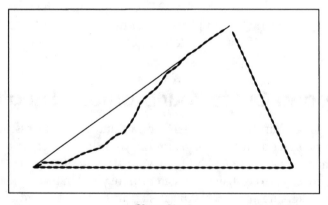

Slow Start

I experienced this kind of roller-coaster ride when I saw *Dead Again*. Even though I eventually became quite hooked, it took a while for my emotional build to start. The moment Kenneth Branagh's character accidentally called Emma Thomson the name from her previous life was an electrifying moment, but it came fairly far into the story.

This kind of structural flaw is due to a problem in bonding with the plot or the characters; it can also be caused by a lack of clear direction. Something in the way the story is being told isn't compelling enough to help the audience get past their resistance and on board the roller coaster, so listen carefully to your instincts and the feedback of others about what might be causing that resistance.

2. Flatlining

This kind of structural problem occurs when a roller coaster works well for a while, but then the pillars begin missing the bell, and eventually the entire roller-coaster structure loses upward build or forward momentum.

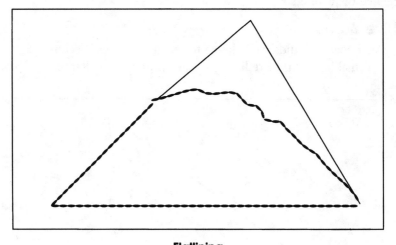

Flatlining

Ironically, the film *Flatliners* created exactly this kind of roller coaster for me. The first near-death experience was fascinating, and the second was also interesting. But after a while, the various experiences failed to be significantly different, and eventually I lost interest in their overall impact because there wasn't enough new information. As with most structurally flatlining stories, they don't really flatline, they actually decline because of the cumulative audience disappointment.

Flatlining usually is caused by problems with new information, especially in the areas of exciting plot complications or richer character reactions. Make sure that you're giving the hero new obstacles and challenges, not just more of the same.

3. Swiss Cheese

This kind of structural problem occurs when the roller-coaster ride works well for a while, then suddenly becomes very wobbly, then stabilizes again. These interruptions can be repeated several times within the story.

As an example, a light love scene just before the climax of the same scene could destroy the overall emotional build because the dramatic stakes aren't high enough.

This kind of structural problem tends to be a problem with conflict resolution because the audience feels that either the plot logic or the character's emotional arc isn't tracking. It can also be caused by problems with subplots and secondary characters who either overwhelm the main story or are not well integrated or justified.

4. Dive-Bomb

This roller coaster builds well almost to the climax, then becomes contrived and implausible, and the credibility of the entire story collapses.

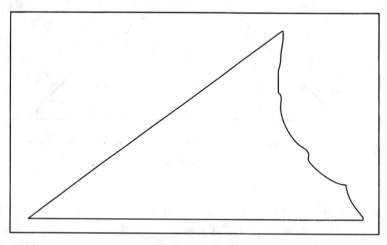

Dive Bomb

This tends to be a problem with completion. The sinking sensation is caused by an unconvincing ending, so examine whether the actual pivotal moment, climax, and end result seem too contrived, whether it's failing to resolve all the problems your story has presented, or if the problem is simply that the audience hasn't been given enough setups to make the final payoffs work.

▪ Decide Where to Fix ▪

It's usually not too hard to tell where the problems are. But where you notice a problem and where the problem is caused aren't always the same thing.

For example, let's say you've given your script to three different readers, and they all feel that there is a scene, just before the climax, where the hero's actions are implausible or unjustified. Your roller coaster has a Swiss cheese problem; and if you were going to graph that roller coaster, it would look something like this:

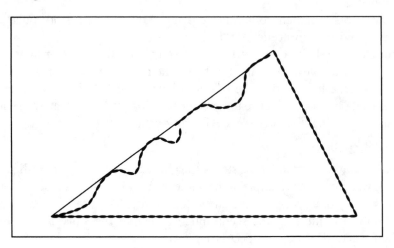

As a result, many writers would automatically begin to rewrite the scene where the sag is evident. However, the reason the scene is not working may have nothing to do with the way that it is written. Because of the cumulative impact of story information, the problem may occur much earlier in the story. Usually the power of the moment comes from what the audience already knows or cares about in the script, so you need to back up and learn *why* they don't like the character. Try to get at the cause of the dissatisfaction.

First identify the location of the problem, and then ask "Why?" *Where* gives you the X-marks-the-spot, and *why* is the clue as to what element is not working. Once this is identified, you can go back and ask, "What if the character did this or said that?" Always try to fix the problem as early as possible, before the audience's cumulative frustration or confusion has a chance to build and interfere with their experience of your story.

▪ Decide How to Fix ▪

When a roller coaster isn't working, it's because the pillars aren't as high as the author expected them to be, so there are four things that you can do with your story pillars to make that section of roller coaster maintain the right height. You can *add, subtract, switch the order*, or *rebuild pillars* in a way to strengthen the emotional experience for the audience.

Here are examples of the four basic options you can consider as you try to strengthen your roller coaster:

1. Adding

One way to strengthen your roller coaster is by adding a story pillar that contains information needed for a later scene to work.

For example, let's say that several people tell you that a major fight scene between a couple isn't working for them. The reason might be that you have failed to make it clear that the husband has a long history of being overly possessive. Once the audience understands the magnitude of that issue within the marriage, then the later scene will work well.

2. Subtracting

Another way to fix a roller coaster is to subtract information from the audience's awareness. For example, if the audience is failing to be surprised by the big discovery of a syringe in the suspected murderer's closet, then a possible solution is to eliminate the scene much earlier in the story in which the audience is told that the suspect is a diabetic.

Another reason to eliminate something from your script is if it snags your attention in a way that distracts from the story. Somerset Maugham was quoted as saying, "Cut if at all possible." If it bothers you, trust your instincts. Anything that can be cut should be cut in order to keep momentum going.

3. Switching Order

The point of switching pillars is that sometimes the same story information, given in a different order, can have greater impact for the audience. Often the order is more a matter of preference. One television producer I've worked with preferred to surprise the audience with the arrival of the police during a crime scene, while his partner preferred to cut away to the cops at intervals to heighten the tension of whether the cops and crooks would meet up. Neither way is "right"; each creates very different sensations in the audience and demands an entirely different storytelling technique. Be aware of the subtleties of sequence; consider alternatives, and ask yourself which way would work better for your script. Pay close attention to this dynamic especially if there is a segment where the feedback you've had suggests that the roller coaster dips around that point. Changing the order of events may just solve the problem.

4. Rebuilding

Sometimes the information you've decided to tell the audience is the right information, but your readers do not understand what's happening because of the way the scene is written. Another possibility is that the moment is more ambiguous than you intended. Or perhaps, even, your readers are misunderstanding what you meant to imply. In such cases, just rewrite the same scene in a less confusing way.

This is an important point because sometimes writers think the comment "I don't understand" means "I don't agree with the character's motivation or the plot's logistics"; it often just means "I don't understand the meaning of that line," or "I am not comprehending the logistics of this sequence."

▪ Easy Doesn't Mean Good ▪

Never make the mistake of thinking that there is a direct correlation between how easy it is for you to get your story on paper and how good a writer you are. Just because it's hard for you doesn't mean that you aren't talented, and just because it comes easily doesn't mean that you are good. I know tremendously talented writers who agonize over every word and take months to finish a screenplay, and I also know writers who can knock off a script in a weekend but who do very ordinary work.

The only thing that determines whether you are a good writer is what ends up on the page at the end of the process. All the rest of it—the long nights of creative angst, the indecision, the confusion—are just your creative "modus operandi," something you may or may not be able to change easily but which usually doesn't matter to the outside world (except maybe friends and family!) as long as you can finally produce a strong script.

Another reason not to get too frustrated if some aspect of screenwriting is hard is that most writers have difficulty with at least one aspect no matter how easily the rest of it comes. The only thing you need to do is be honest with yourself, know your strengths and weaknesses so that you can take them into account when you are scheduling a deadline, and try to focus on trusting the process.

▪ Don't Hurry Past the Discomfort ▪

The reason many writers fail to write a great script is because they simply aren't willing to stay in the emotional and intellectual stage of discomfort long enough to find the right creative solution for their story.

So rather than worrying about how hard it is for you at moments, all you have to worry about is your own tolerance for discomfort. It's very tempting to skip whatever part of the rewriting process is hard for you. Many writers respond to creative panic by obsessively worrying about some minor point; they think that their specific concern is the issues, but often it's really that they don't trust their own creative process. For example, they rework their ending when they should be carefully examining their foundation, and thus they miss the chance to fine-tune each layer of the story as it develops. Instead of staying with the discomfort until they find a creative solution that really feels right, writers often cheat themselves out of the satisfaction of finding just the right balance, pacing, whatever, because they don't take long enough to do the homework.

Ironically, charging past the real complexities of the creative process too quickly forces writers to forgo exactly the clarity they are so hungry for. In the effort to have a sense of security, they pass up the chance to obtain true success.

FINAL QUESTIONS

1. What feedback have you gotten on your roller coaster?
2. Does your roller coaster capture your dramatic center?
3. Does your roller coaster convey your dramatic equation?
4. Which category would most of your notes fall into?
    New information?
    Bonding?
    Conflict resolution?
    Completion?
5. Where in the script are most problems located?
6. If you were going to graph it, how would it look?
    Slow start?
    Flatlining?
    Swiss cheese?
    Dive-bomb?
7. Which techniques would strengthen your roller coaster?
    Adding pillars?
    Subtracting?
    Switching?
    Rebuilding?

FIFTEEN

Final Words

I had a theater professor who used to say, "Don't go into theater unless there's nothing else you can stand to do!" It drove me crazy at the time, but now I know why he was so insistent. Show business is a rough business, and there are few occupations with more potential for hard work and disappointment. Even being at the top it is a bumpy ride, and struggling to get there can be very tough indeed.

So my advice to you is don't decide that screenwriting is a quick and easy way to fame and fortune. In fact, don't do it for the money or the glamour or the power or for any other reason if you don't have a passion for the work. Do it for the story. For the product. For the process. For the truths in you that must be told.

 Every society has its storytellers and, more important, *needs* its storytellers. Being a storyteller is an ancient and honorable role, one that provides an important service to society. This century the media have been film and television, but the function and the societal needs have been the same in every other period in history.

■ 187 ■

Final Words

In fact, some people say that stories are all the philosophy that most humans will ever experience. People certainly don't make much time to read Nietzsche or Hume, Einstein or Freud. But what they do make time for are stories. Films. TV. Soap operas. Sitcoms. Movies of the Week. In the continuous effort "to make life make sense," people reach for stories. To obtain catharsis. Clarity. Affirmation. Enjoyment. Release.

Look at the impact the entertainment industry has had. Archie Bunker's chair is in the Smithsonian. *M.A.S.H.* helped the peace movement coalesce. Fashion was dominated by the torn sweatshirts of *Flashdance* and the goofy sweetness of *Annie Hall*. *JFK* got sealed government files opened, and *The Burning Bed* brought wife abuse to a new height of national consciousness. Stories have impact, intended or not.

Until recently, daily life provided many opportunities for such venting and catharsis. Babies were born at home, and the dead were laid out in the next room until the burial. However, modern society has removed most people from such natural occurrences and so emotions build up with few avenues for release. Yet the primal needs remain. If people don't find appropriate outlets, they will create some other way to vent those feelings—through violence, chemical addiction, or resignation and stagnation.

Yet in addition to their yearning for catharsis, people also need inspiration. They need role models of courage and greatness, happiness and wholeness. The specifics of the challenge each human faces may differ, but the underlying fundamentals of life, birth, death, loss, and success will never change. What changes is how the audience learns to see and value them. As one of society's storytellers, you must learn how to express what they mean to you.

So be bold. Be daring. Don't follow formulas. Don't build the same roller coaster again and again. The one thing you have to offer is your voice, your perceptions. The entertainment business needs great stories, films, and television shows that thrill, move, enlighten, delight, that create vivid adventures for the audience's minds, emotions, and souls. That kind of "soul contact" is not possible without the passion, imagination, and originality that each writer has to contribute.

That's why Hollywood needs you. This book is dedicated to the goal of helping you gain access to the highest level of creativity and craft of which you are capable, in the deep and fervent belief that the world needs to hear what you need to say.

Final Words

IF YOU ARE INTERESTED IN ORGANIZING
A CLASS OR SEMINAR WITH THE AUTHOR,
PLEASE CONTACT:

DONA COOPER
at THE AMERICAN FILM INSTITUTE,
2021 N. WESTERN AVENUE,
LOS ANGELES, CA 90027